D0042721

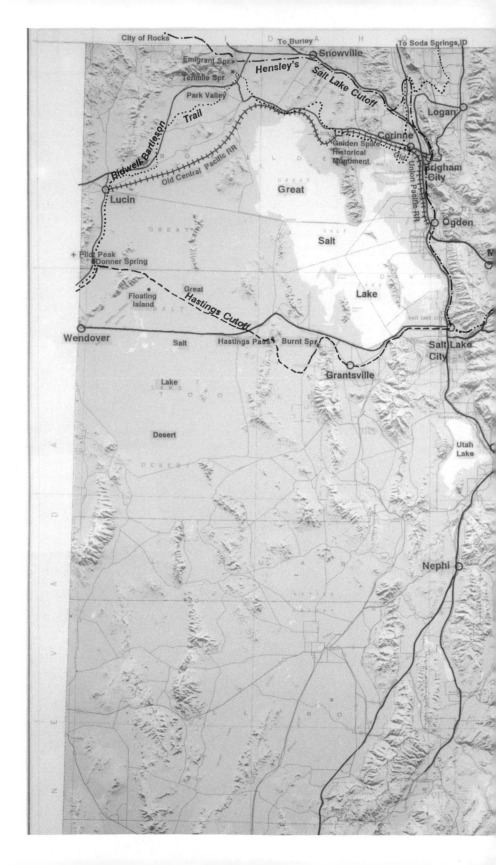

Trailing the Pioneers

Northern Utah

Bidwell-Bartleson Trail ·······················

Hastings Cutoff ~~~~~~~~~~~

Hensley's Salt Lake Cutoff ~·~·~·~·~·

Pioneer Trail ~·~·~·~·~·~·

Ft. Bridger

Evanston,WY

Cache Cave — Pioneer Trail

Echo Canyon

Echo

W Y O M I N G

U I N T A

B A S I N

Price

C O L O R A D O

TRAILING THE PIONEERS

To Utah's four pioneering trail historians:

Charles Kelly (1889–1971)
Photograph Archives, Utah State Historical Society

J. Roderic Korns (1890–1949)
Photograph Archives, Utah State Historical Society

David E. Miller (1909–1978)
Photograph Archives, Utah State Historical Society

Dale L. Morgan (1914–1971)
Photograph by Harold Schindler

TRAILING THE
PIONEERS

*A Guide
to Utah's Emigrant Trails,
1829–1869*

edited by
Peter H. DeLafosse

Utah State University Press, *with*
Utah Crossroads, Oregon-California Trails Association

LOGAN, UTAH
1994

Utah State University Press
Logan, Utah 84322-7800

LIBRARY OF CONGRESS CATALOGING-IN-PUBLICATION DATA

Trailing the pioneers: a guide to Utah's emigrant trails, 1829–1869
  edited by Peter H. DeLafosse
  p.   cm.
  Includes bibliographic references and index.
  ISBN 0-87421-175-1 (cloth: acid-free).
  ISBN 0-87421-172-7 (paper: acid-free).
  1. Trails — Utah — Guidebooks. 2. Utah — Guidebooks.
  3. Utah — History, Local. 4. Historic sites — Utah — Guidebooks.
  I. DeLafosse, Peter H., 1947–
  F824.3.T73 1994
  917.9204'33 — dc20   94-825
                                                          CIP

Contents

~~~

ACKNOWLEDGMENTS   vi

FOREWORD   vii

INTRODUCTION   by Peter H. DeLafosse   1

THE SPANISH TRAIL   by Steven K. Madsen   9
   Utah–Colorado Border to Green River, Utah   12
   Green River to Salina, Utah   18
   Salina to Cedar City, Utah   23
   Cedar City to Utah–Arizona Border   27

THE BIDWELL-BARTLESON TRAIL   by Roy D. Tea   33
   Soda Springs, Idaho to Corinne, Utah   35
   Corinne to Wendover, Utah   44

THE PIONEER TRAIL   by Jack B. Tykal   55
   Fort Bridger, Wyoming to Salt Lake City   58

THE HASTINGS CUTOFF   by Rush Spedden   73
   Salt Lake City to Wendover, Utah   76

HENSLEY'S SALT LAKE CUTOFF   by Will Bagley   93
   Salt Lake City to City of Rocks, Idaho   98

SELECTED BIBLIOGRAPHY   by Harold Schindler   111

INDEX   123

Acknowledgments

~~~

We acknowledge the financial support of the Utah State Historical Society through its Local History Grants Program, and thank Max J. Evans, director of the Utah State Historical Society and Jay M. Haymond, coordinator of the Local History Grant, for their support. We acknowledge also the financial support of the Marriott Library at the University of Utah, and thank Roger K. Hanson, director of libraries, and Gregory C. Thompson, assistant director, for their support. Special thanks are due David L. Bigler, Floyd A. O'Neil, and W. L. Rusho for reading early drafts of the manuscript and for many suggested improvements and John Alley, Utah State University Press editor, and Albert Mulder, Jr., president of Utah Crossroads, for their advice and support.

Foreword

~~~

Utah Crossroads is proud to present this new guidebook to the historic emigrant trails of our state as a special offering of the 1994 convention of the Oregon-California Trails Association at Salt Lake City and as a unique contribution to our 1996 Utah Statehood Centennial. This work combines many years of research and field study by some of the foremost authorities on these trails, members of our OCTA chapter. It is offered to the public by the men and women of Utah Crossroads, who are dedicated to the identification and preservation of Utah's historic routes of exploration, trade, and emigration.

Albert Mulder, Jr.
President
Utah Crossroads
Oregon-California Trails Association

Introduction

Peter H. DeLafosse

❧

ABOUT THIS BOOK

On their way to California in 1841, the Bidwell-Bartleson party separated from their traveling companions at what is now Soda Springs, Idaho. Heading south and entering Cache Valley, they brought the first wagons into present-day Utah. A flood of emigrants followed over the next decade, establishing the routes of Utah's great overland trails. The overland emigrants were searching for many things — land, religious sanctuary, gold, a new beginning — and the trails they developed united the Atlantic and Pacific oceans. Utah was at the crossroads of this travel.

Trailing the Pioneers is a concise guide to Utah's emigrant trails during the years 1829 to 1869. This four-decade period opened with the establishment of a trade route from Santa Fe to southern California that passed through Utah; included the period of heavy overland travel to Oregon and California in the 1840s and 1850s, the arrival of the Mormon pioneers in 1847, and the Mormon colonization of the Intermountain West; and closed with the completion of the transcontinental railroad in 1869, the symbolic end of overland wagon travel. This period left a rich historical legacy, much of which can be seen from today's roads.

Comprising a series of automobile tours, this book is intended for the general tourist traveling in an ordinary passenger car. The tours include directions to view trail remnants, and a few optional offroad vehicle tours for those interested in exploring remote sections of the trails. The trails include

- The Spanish Trail from the Utah-Colorado border, near Monticello, to the Utah-Arizona border, near St. George;
- The Bidwell-Bartleson Trail from Soda Springs, Idaho, to Wendover, Utah;
- The Pioneer Trail from Fort Bridger, Wyoming, to Salt Lake City;
- The Hastings Cutoff from Salt Lake City to Wendover, Utah; and
- The Salt Lake Cutoff from Salt Lake City to City of Rocks, Idaho.

Prefacing each tour is a brief historical perspective, followed by the tour description, which attempts to answer questions such as Why did the emigrants follow this particular route? What obstacles did the emigrants face? and Which trail landmarks did the emigrants consider important enough to record in their journals? Written in an informal style, each tour description includes an approximation of the route of the trail using today's roads, identifies the location of the actual trail in relationship to the roads, and interprets the trail's history.

Obviously, the information in a book of this size must be selective. The tours are designed to give you a sense of the epic sweep of the trail and an awareness of the major landmarks noted by the pioneers. Trail enthusiasts will want to explore the vast trail literature, and the selected bibliography will give you an introduction to primary and secondary sources of information on the trails included in this book.

ORGANIZATION AND MODEL

Trailing the Pioneers is cast in the tradition of the American Guide Series published in the 1930s and 1940s by the Federal Writers' Project of the Work Projects Administration (WPA). The Federal Writers' Project provided work for unemployed writers during the Great Depression. Under this program, writers gathered local historical material into state archives, preserving much information that would otherwise have been lost, and a guidebook was written and published for each state.

State guidebooks were divided into two parts. The first consisted of a series of essays about the state's history, peoples, geography, and natural resources. The second comprised a series of automobile tours along the state's major roads. The tours interpreted the view as seen by the automobile tourist, identifying towns, major points of interest, and items of historical importance. The informal style of the automobile tours, mixing historical fact and anecdote, contributed to their charm.

The Idaho and Utah guidebooks were among the best written volumes of this American Guide Series. Idaho novelist Vardis Fisher was appointed state director of the Idaho Writers' Project in 1935, and under his capable leadership, *Idaho: A Guide in Word and Picture* was published in January 1937. The first volume published in the American Guide Series, the Idaho guide set the organizational standard for the succeeding volumes.

Utah was most fortunate in having native son Dale L. Morgan as state supervisor of the Utah Writers' Program. Under Morgan's direction and following the organizational model of the Idaho guide (general essays followed by tours), *Utah: A Guide to the State* was published in 1941. The Utah guide bears Morgan's personal stamp because, like Fisher, he wrote most of the text. It was Morgan's first major book and launched his distinguished career as a western historian.

The American Guide Series volumes contain much valuable information, but in the half-century since their appearance new information has been discovered that needs to be documented in a convenient and accessible form. This was one of our objectives in writing *Trailing the Pioneers*. In instances where details remain in dispute, it is so noted, and we welcome corrections for future editions.

TRAIL NAMES

Utah's emigrant trails existed in both place and time, and their names may be confusing because trails sometimes overlapped. Naming the trail from Fort Bridger to Salt Lake City poses a particular problem. Pioneering this route in 1846 were several emigrant groups — including the Bryant-Russell, Harlan-Young, and Donner-Reed parties — on their way to California via the Hastings Cutoff across the Great Salt Lake Desert. The Mormons followed this route to Salt Lake Valley in 1847 at the end of their trek from Nauvoo, Illinois. By 1850, the trail had become a well-traveled road, serving as the eastern end of the Hastings Cutoff, the eastern approach to the Salt Lake Cutoff, and the western end of the Mormon Trail. In the context of this book, Pioneer Trail designates the route from Fort Bridger to Salt Lake City, and Hastings Cutoff designates the route from Salt Lake City to Pilot Peak.

3

Emigrant trails differ from our modern concept of a highway — a well-defined roadbed. Emigrant trails sometimes had variant routes for part of their distance. Again using the Pioneer Trail example, the Bryant-Russell and Harlan-Young parties traveled from Fort Bridger to Salt Lake City via Weber Canyon, while the Donner-Reed party and the Mormon pioneers traveled to Salt Lake City via Emigration Canyon. The Pioneer Trail, as described here, includes these two variant routes.

IMPORTANCE OF UTAH'S HISTORIC TRAILS

Why is it important to view the trails? Describing Jedediah Smith's 1827 trek across the Great Salt Lake Desert, Utah historian Charles Kelly wrote, "This expedition of Jedediah Smith in crossing such a barren and desolate country for the first time, without any knowledge whatever of what lay before him, has never been fully appreciated by historians, due partly to his own brief account of the journey, and partly to the historians' lack of first-hand knowledge of the country over which he had to pass." Many historians now understand and appreciate the experience of early travelers, but one can achieve a clear understanding of the written record only by seeing the landscape through which the emigrants traveled. Unlike the written record, which is subject to archival preservation, trails are ephemeral. Modern roads and development projects have obliterated many trail segments. Ultimately, nature will reclaim all trail remnants. However, overland emigrant history is relatively recent, presenting us with the opportunity to study the trails firsthand.

Published in 1930, Charles Kelly's *Salt Desert Trails: A History of the Hastings Cutoff and Other Early Trails Which Crossed the Great Salt Desert Seeking a Shorter Road to California* was one of the first books to awaken modern interest in Utah's trails. Kelly's magnificent black and white photographs, which illustrate *Salt Desert Trails*, capture like no other images the awesome loneliness, desolation, and grandeur of the Great Salt Lake Desert, so vividly noted in emigrant journals. Kelly described his personal travels across the desert in the last chapter of his book, to which he gave the title "Trailing the Pioneers." We pay tribute to Kelly's pioneering research by borrowing his chapter title for the title of this book.

ABOUT THE AUTHORS

Trailing the Pioneers is the premier publication of the Utah Crossroads chapter of the Oregon-California Trails Association (OCTA). Founded in 1982 and headquartered in Independence, Missouri, OCTA is a nonprofit organization dedicated to the preservation and appreciation of all trans-Mississippi emigrant trails to the American West. OCTA supports trail identification and marking and encourages trail studies through its publications and educational programs. *Overland Journal* is OCTA's quarterly magazine and contains scholarly articles and book reviews about historic trails. *News from the Plains* is OCTA's quarterly newsletter and provides information about national and local OCTA activities. Annual conventions are held during the second week in August and include presentations of papers, educational workshops, and field trips near the host city. Local OCTA chapters sponsor regional field trips and other activities. Utah Crossroads was organized in January, 1990.

The authors and editor of *Trailing the Pioneers* are all charter members of Utah Crossroads. Peter DeLafosse received his bachelor's degree in engineering sciences from Purdue University and is employed by Evans & Sutherland Computer Corporation. He is a member of the Utah Westerners and the Utah State Historical Society and is the co-author of *Utah Westerners Calendar of Events* (1990). Peter serves on the Utah Westerners board of directors and is secretary of the organization.

Will Bagley received his bachelor's degree in history from the University of California at Santa Cruz. In 1969, he built a raft in Rock Island, Illinois, and took it 1,300 miles down the Mississippi River to New Orleans, visiting historic sites along the way. He has edited *A Road from El Dorado: The 1848 Trail Journal of Ephraim Green* (1991) and *Frontiersman: Abner Blackburn's Narrative* (1992). *Frontiersman* was awarded the 1991 Evans Biography Award by the Mountain West Center for Regional Studies. Will is a national director of OCTA and is a member of Utah Westerners, the Utah State Historical Society, the Mormon History Association, and the Western History Association.

Steven K. Madsen is the historian of Washington, D.C.'s National Independence Day Festival and Parade. He received his bachelor's degree from the University of Utah and his master's degree from Brigham Young University. He is responsible for the recent discovery and unearthing of the historic Union Fort wall south of Salt Lake City. He is the author of *A Union, Utah, History; Precinct Government in Salt Lake County, Utah*; and the government studies *Boating on the Upper Colorado* and *The Navigational History of Bear River*. He co-authored with Dr. C. Gregory Crampton the forthcoming book *In Search of the Spanish Trail, Santa Fe to L.A.* Steven is a member of Utah Westerners and a life member of the Sons of the Utah Pioneers. In 1982, America the Beautiful Fund of Washington, D.C., awarded him the National Good Citizen Award for his efforts in preserving the Union Pioneer Cemetery.

Harold Schindler is daily columnist and feature writer for *The Salt Lake Tribune*. He is the author of *Orrin Porter Rockwell: Man of God, Son of Thunder* and is the winner of the American Association for State and Local History Award of Merit in 1967 for Outstanding Contribution to Local History. He is a founder and charter vice president of Utah Westerners, has been a member of the Utah State Historical Society Advisory Board of Editors since 1970, and was named an Honorary Life Member of the Utah State Historical Society in 1992 for distinguished service. Harold received the Dominguez-Escalante State/Federal Bicentennial Committee Newspaper Publications Award in 1976. He was contributing commentator on PBS's "The American Experience: The Donner Party."

Rush Spedden is a retired consulting mining engineer. He received his bachelor's degree in mining engineering from the University of Washington and his master's degree in mineral processing from the Montana School of Mines. He worked in Bolivia as an engineer for the United States Government, and then served in the United States Army in Europe. After World War II, he taught at MIT and later was a research director for Union Carbide in New York and then for Kennecott Copper Corporation in Salt Lake City. He is the author of numerous technical papers and patents in the field of mineral processing. He is the past president of the Society of Mining Engineers of the American Institute of Mining, Metallurgical and Petroleum Engineers, as well as 1968 president of the International Mineral Processing Congress. He is the author of "Who Was T. H. Jefferson," *Overland Journal* (1990). Rush is a member of Utah Westerners.

Roy Tea is a retired engineer from the Utah State Department of Transportation. Following service in the army, he received his bachelor's degree in geology from Brigham Young University. He was employed by the Utah State Department of Transportation for thirty-five years, obtained his professional engineer's license, and worked on highway location and as a materials engineer. During his work on the Bonneville Salt Flats, he discovered the historic Hastings and Donner-Reed trail, and spent his spare time over the next thirty years locating, following, and marking it, especially during the year preceding the flooding of the trail from the Great Salt Lake high-water pumping project. Roy is a member of the newly formed Lincoln Highway Association.

Jack Tykal is retired from the Federal Bureau of Investigation. He received his bachelor's degree in history and political science from De-Pauw University. He joined the FBI as a special agent. His FBI work took him to Atlanta, Monterey (California), Washington, D.C., and finally Salt Lake City, where he served as assistant special agent in charge before his retirement. Jack is a member of Utah Westerners and has served on the board of directors and as vice president. He is the author of *Etienne Provost: Man of the Mountains* (1989), "Etienne Provost and the Hawken Rifle," *Museum of the Fur Trade Quarterly* (1990), and "Taos to St. Louis: The Journey of Maria Rosa Villalpando," *New Mexico Historical Review* (1990). He is currently editing an 1841 journal about a buffalo hunt to Kansas, which is scheduled for publication in 1994.

USING THIS BOOK

To help you follow the routes, important landmarks, points of inter-est, and direction changes are indicated by CAPITAL LETTERS. Mileages in parentheses following a LANDMARK are cumulative from the previous LANDMARK. Unless noted in context, interim mileages are cumulative to the next LANDMARK. Automobile odometers may differ, so mileages may vary. Do not rely totally on mileages to locate the routes. Look for landmarks, and, above all, use the maps.

Roads are designated as follows:

I	Interstate Route
US	U.S. Route
SR	State Route
CR	County Route

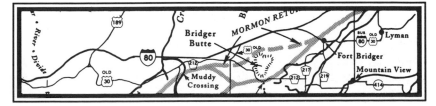

When traveling in desolate desert country, you should always follow these common sense precautions:

- Check local road conditions before starting,
- Carry plenty of food and water,
- Secure proper authorization before entering private land,
- Make sure you have a spare tire and the equipment to make tire changes,
- If possible, arrange to travel with other vehicles, and
- Inform a friend or relative of your travel plans and expected time of return.

Remember, not all segments of the trails are accessible to the general public. You should respect the privacy of property owners.

The Spanish Trail

Steven K. Madsen

Casa Colorado, named for its unusual house-like form, dominates the landscape alongside the Spanish Trail. *Photograph by Steven K. Madsen.*

HISTORICAL PERSPECTIVE

The Spanish Trail — the first commercial route to span the greater part of the American Southwest — followed a large northward-looping course that passed through the rugged southern and central landscapes of Utah. Those who rode the trail avoided the deep river canyons of the Colorado and the hostile Indians that occupied the long, dry stretches across Arizona. The 1,120-mile route, from Santa Fe, New Mexico, to Los Angeles, California, took trail riders over two months to complete.

Arcing northward into the Colorado Plateau from the upper Rio Grande, the Spanish Trail penetrated the redrock canyon country of southeastern Utah. The gorges of the Colorado and Green rivers were obstacles to overland travel. Passage through the region required travelers to ford the major streams at feasible crossings, and the rugged topography dictated their route. The most practicable fording places for the Spanish Trail riders were located where the river canyons open out near today's towns of Moab and Green River, Utah. Here the rivers were easily approachable.

Spaniards laid the groundwork for the Spanish Trail. The eastern segment of the trail, winding through northwestern New Mexico and southwestern Colorado, followed portions of the route taken in 1776 by the Spanish priests Francisco Atanasio Dominguez and Francisco Silvestre Velez de Escalante. Tracing part of the trail explored in 1765 by Juan Maria de Rivera, Dominguez and Escalante were trying to develop a supply route which would connect the northern Spanish outposts in New Mexico and California. Although they failed in their objective, Dominguez and Escalante explored a two-thousand-mile circuitous course, returning to their base at Santa Fe. They were the first Europeans to explore the region of Utah.

In 1776, another Franciscan, Francisco Tomas Hermenegildo Garces, sought a route between California and New Mexico. His attempt also proved unsuccessful. Nevertheless, he managed to explore a segment of the Spanish Trail along the Mojave River in California.

After these explorations, other Spanish parties apparently traveled along segments of what later became the Spanish Trail to carry on trade with the Indians living along Utah's Wasatch Front. In 1827, Jedediah Smith connected the traces made by Dominguez-Escalante and Garces when he made an overland trek from the mountain wilderness of the West to southern California.

Soon after Mexico laid claim to the Southwest, wool merchants and fur trappers blazed the Spanish Trail route, which did not reach as far north as Dominguez and Escalante had. Although later American explorers dubbed it Spanish, the full route was in use only during the Mexican period, from 1829 to 1848. It carried New Mexican pack trains, loaded with woolen goods — blankets, serapes, rugs, leggings, and yardage — from settlements on the upper Rio Grande to the Mexican pueblos of southern California. The annual trade caravans comprised the greatest volume of traffic over the trail. When traders reached the coastal settlements, they exchanged their woven textiles for horses and mules. Returning parties then drove upwards of two thousand animals back over the trail to Santa Fe.

The Spanish Trail experienced heavy use during its twenty-year history, but there are few contemporary descriptions of the route. A lawyer named Orville C. Pratt was the only traveler who kept a diary of travel along the entire trail from New Mexico to California. To verify the route, therefore, we must rely on additional sources. Much of what we know comes to us from the writings of travelers in post-trail days who were aware they were traversing the Spanish Trail. Many of them were following only segments of the historic route. Nevertheless, their observations help us identify its location.

During the course of his second expedition for the federal government, John Charles Frémont followed the western section of the Spanish Trail from Cajon Pass in California to Little Salt Lake in Utah. His report and accompanying map were copied by later explorers and became useful references for Americans, including Mormons, who converted the western half of the Spanish Trail into a wagon road between Utah and southern California. This wagon route has been called the Mormon Road, the Old California Road, the Salt Lake Road, the Southern Route, and the Salt Lake to Los Angeles Route.

Paralleling present-day I-15, the Southern Route originated in Salt Lake City and joined the Spanish Trail in Little Salt Lake Valley, near Parowan. The Southern Route continued over the Spanish Trail, or parallel to it, all the way to Los Angeles. Mormon soldiers discharged from the Mexican War were the first to roll a wheeled vehicle over a substantial portion of the trail. The increased traffic over the Southern Route that resulted from the 1849 California gold rush turned the trail into a wagon road. The road was further developed by Mormon colonizers of Las Vegas, Nevada, and San Bernardino, California, in the 1850s, and helped create a Mormon corridor to the Pacific Ocean. Eventually, major highways connecting Salt Lake City with Los Angeles would be built along and over the old wagon tracks.

Much of the Spanish Trail is difficult to locate by a conventional vehicle, and access is limited in remote sections — obstacles to passage are numerous. The automobile tour follows the general route but sometimes parallels the trail at a considerable distance. Because of the extreme length and remote location of the trail, the automobile tour has been divided into four sections: the Utah-Colorado border to Green River, Green River to Salina, Salina to Cedar City, and Cedar City to the Utah-Arizona border. For clarity, each automobile tour section is prefaced by a description of the trail. To give you a sense of the trail's vast 460-mile length in Utah, the mileages listed in these prefatory descriptions are cumulative from the Utah-Colorado border.

UTAH-COLORADO BORDER TO GREEN RIVER, UTAH

Pack trains, trudging along the Spanish Trail over the Great Sage Plain plateau of southwestern Colorado, entered Utah near the present site of Ucolo, a settlement some 15 miles east of Monticello. They were 270 miles from the outfitting point at Santa Fe, nearly one-fourth of their way to Los Angeles. A 460-mile stretch of trail through Utah lay ahead.

Shortly beyond the Utah-Colorado border, riders stopped at an important watering place known today as PIUTE SPRING (2.0 miles). From the 1890s, it was a major campsite on the Monticello-Dolores road, which generally followed the Spanish Trail. Herman U. Butt of Monticello homesteaded the site in 1912–1913. The spring provided abundant supplies of water — enough to develop a modern ranch. From Piute Spring, the trail continued to the Summit area, at the extreme northwestern edge of the Great Sage Plain plateau. Here the trail, by way of SOUTH CANYON (15.0 miles), dropped down a thousand feet to the nearly level floor of EAST CANYON (19.0 miles). The descent into the brilliantly painted canyon was described by trail diarist Orville C. Pratt on 13 September 1848: "We began descending one of the longest and steepest mountains yet passed over. But we got down it with safety. After reaching the bottom the scenery in the valley was the most rugged and sublime I ever beheld."

The Macomb military expedition of 1859 named this colorful canyon Cañon Pintado (Painted Canyon). To survey a wagon road from the Rio

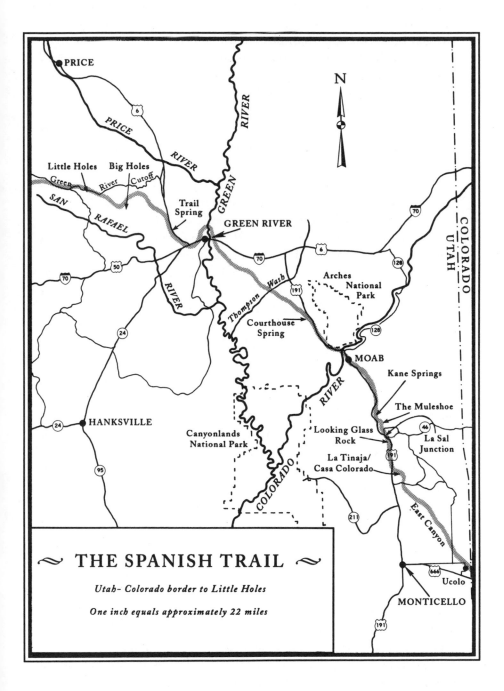

N

~ THE SPANISH TRAIL ~

Utah- Colorado border to Little Holes

One inch equals approximately 22 miles

Grande to Utah's settlements, Captain John N. Macomb of the War Department's Corps of Topographical Engineers followed the well-defined Spanish Trail. Macomb's party marveled at the "intricate mass of irregular bluffs, detached buttes & sinuous canyons" east of today's Canyonlands National Park. The maps and reports created by the expedition accurately document the Spanish Trail throughout much of its eastern half.

Cañon Pintado opens into Dry Valley, an extensive basin punctuated by a variety of redrock monuments and drained by Hatch Wash. Approaching the upper end of the valley, Macomb's party reached a landmark rock over two hundred feet high. The weathered alcoves along its southern face, like the windows of a massive house, suggested the name Casa Colorada (Red House).

The party camped near LA TINAJA (29.0 miles) (The Tank), a dependable water source where nature has carved a series of rock basins into the slickrock base of Casa Colorada. J. S. Newberry, the geologist for the Macomb expedition, described La Tinaja as a "deep excavation in red sandstone, which retains so large a quantity of water and for so long a time as to become an important watering place on the Spanish Trail." Standing on the raised undulating surface at La Tinaja, one can imagine early desert travelers forming "bucket brigades" to haul water in leather buckets from rock reservoirs to thirsty pack animals below the pour-off.

From La Tinaja, trail riders encountered brilliant formations as they followed an easy grade down Hatch Wash. Near US 191 (33.5 miles), between Moab and Monticello, some five miles west of La Tinaja, the trail swung northward, bypassing the eastern fringes of what is now Canyonlands National Park. Here the Macomb party left the trail to explore toward the Colorado River, hoping to find its confluence with the Green River.

West of US 191, and 2.5 miles south of La Sal Junction, travelers on the Spanish Trail passed LOOKING GLASS ROCK (38.8 miles), a landmark standing over one hundred feet high, identified by its large window. A Mormon party sent to explore the region south of Moab in 1855 followed the Spanish Trail past Looking Glass, calling it a "big rock with hole through it." The scouting party continued on to Navajo territory on the San Juan River after leaving the trail to "Santa Fee."

Beyond Looking Glass Rock, the trail threads its way through a rugged passage that extends toward Moab. The big cattle companies, established in southeastern Utah beginning in the early 1880s, drove their livestock over this stretch of the Spanish Trail to shipping points north of Moab. On the desert drive, cattlemen often "nooned" at a formation four hundred feet high topped by round-shaped rocks, imaginatively named the Nipples. Plodding over the arid range, they moved their herds four miles to MULESHOE CANYON (45.8 miles). Here the trail took the shape of a large muleshoe as it looped sharply to ascend the rim of the steep defile, descended and crossed the canyon where the walls diminish, then turned back along the opposite rim.

The cowboys pushed their cattle beyond the Muleshoe, brushing against the hot, sunlit walls of the towering sandstone bluffs. Cattlemen remember it as the hottest place on the drive, where cattle's tongues distended as they hastened to reach the springs beyond a massive protruding rock, ST. LOUIS ROCK (48.3 miles), named by the 1855 Mormon scouting party. Today this rock, jutting against US 191, is covered by commercial graffiti and the inscriptions of passersby.

Thirsty cattle herds drank from the abundant waters of KANE (or Cane) SPRINGS (48.8 miles), in the shadow of St. Louis Rock. Trail diarist Orville Pratt, in 1848, referred to this flow of water as the Corasito, an archaic word whose meaning remains a mystery. This historic campsite on the Spanish Trail is now a highway rest stop, and the spring water continues to refresh weary travelers.

Pulling out of Kane Springs Canyon, trail riders climbed a steep, rocky path cut into the hillside east of the present highway, to the top of Blue Hill. The narrow, precipitous DUGWAY (49.5 miles), to the east is still visible, providing motorists with a glimpse of the Spanish Trail. From this point, the trail made a long, rugged drop, roughly paralleling US 191, to the head of Spanish Valley.

Flanked by high redrock cliffs, travelers passed through Spanish Valley's natural funnel on their way to the Colorado River. Early parties followed Pack Creek and Mill Creek over the level floor of the valley, in full view of the majestic peaks of the La Sal (Salt) Mountains. Orville Pratt's party made camp in 1848 on the "good grass and water" of Pack Creek, then called Salt Creek since it originated in the La Sal Mountains.

On the southern approach to the Colorado River the Spanish Trail passes through the modern tourist capital at MOAB (64.5 miles).

Beyond Spanish Valley, the trail reached the Colorado River by way of Moab Valley, its natural extension. Striking the south bank of the Colorado, Orville Pratt found the river swollen from recent rains. Pratt's party wasted little time constructing a crude raft to convey goods and equipment to the opposite bank. Then men and animals swam across the swift stream, "the most rapid for its size I ever saw," according to Pratt. He placed the crossing six hundred yards above "a deep canyon" (the Portal).

The more favorable crossing lies upstream, about one-half mile below the present highway bridge. C. S. Cecil Thompson, a regional transportation authority, identified for the author the north bank approach to the ford between the uranium mill and the mouth of Courthouse Wash. The channel is 250 yards wide at the crossing. At low water, travelers crossed on a firm bottom to the opposite bank, passing over an exposed island in the middle.

The trail through here, opened by Ute Indians, was a thoroughfare for fur traders and mountain men on their way to the upper drainage of the Green River. After crossing the Colorado, trappers spread across the country that opens to the north, sometimes leaving inscriptions on canyon walls of the region to mark their passage.

After fording the COLORADO RIVER (67.5 miles), travelers found spectacular trailside scenery as they entered Moab Canyon and worked their way north. Moving up the canyon, today's explorers will encounter Arches National Park, which contains a segment of the Spanish Trail. A grand array of formations drenched in rich russet tones, including many finely sculpted arches and windows, lure today's trail followers to the inner reaches of the park. Above the entrance to Arches, early travelers continued their climb within the spreading walls of Moab Canyon, affording extraordinary views of eroded cliffs.

The trail topped out at UPPER COURTHOUSE SPRING (79.3 miles), about twelve miles beyond the Colorado River. Orville Pratt described the spring, used today to water livestock, as a "small run of living water."

The trail then followed a northwest path across the wide Green River Desert. Only the Book and Roan cliffs on the northern skyline broke the monotonous, barren landscape lying ahead. In September 1853, midway across the desert, the Gunnison railroad survey party intersected the Spanish Trail and followed it twenty miles west and north to the GREEN RIVER CROSSING (112.5 miles). Here, camped on the opposite bank of the Green, was a band of Akanaquint, or Green River, Indians. The Indians crossed the stream at the historic Spanish Trail ford to carry on trade with Gunnison's men. Using distances published in

Gunnison's survey report and information supplied by later travelers, we know the crossing was 3.5 miles above the highway bridge near the John Wesley Powell River History Museum.

John Wesley Powell came through the Green River area on both of his epic voyages to explore the Green and Colorado rivers. On his first expedition, in 1869, Powell made a noon stop at the Old Spanish Crossing before launching down the Green. When his party camped near here on the second voyage in 1871, Powell renamed the crossing after John Gunnison.

The automobile tour starts at the JUNCTION of the Utah-Colorado border and US 666, east of the town of Monticello. Monticello is located in southeastern Utah, 291 miles from Salt Lake City.

From the Utah-Colorado border, travel west on US 666. At 1.2 miles is a junction with a road heading north to the small town of Ucolo, the approximate point at which the Spanish Trail entered Utah. Continue west to MONTICELLO (17.0 miles). The town was named for President Thomas Jefferson's home, but it is pronounced "Montisello."

From Monticello, travel north on US 191 through Peters Canyon. In the distance, west of US 191, are the Abajo Mountains, known locally as the Blue Mountains. Descending Peters Canyon, you drop from the Great Sage Plain — a southward sloping plateau extending from Mesa Verde to the Abajo Mountains — into the spectacular redrock canyon country of southeastern Utah.

At 20.0 miles is the junction with the Needles Overlook road on the left.

Optional tour to Casa Colorado and La Tinaja. Approximately 2.0 miles beyond the Needles Overlook road is the junction with a paved road on the right. Follow this paved road east 4.0 miles to CASA COLORADO, an imposing sandstone formation along the Spanish Trail. Hike the jeep trail to the south side of Casa Colorado, where you will find LA TINAJA, the large natural tanks carved into the slickrock base of Casa Colorado.
Return to US 191.

Continue north to LA SAL JUNCTION (32.0 miles). At 4.0 miles is Muleshoe Canyon, where the Spanish Trail took the shape of a large muleshoe as it crossed the canyon east of US 191. At 6.3 miles is St. Louis Rock, a commercial landmark known today as Hole 'N the Rock. Just north of St. Louis Rock is a highway rest stop at the site of Kane Springs on the Spanish Trail. North of the Kane Springs rest stop 1.1

miles is a segment of the Spanish Trail heading east from US 191. This trail near the summit of the hill, known locally as Blue Hill, was widened later into a wagon road and can still be seen today.

Continue north to MOAB (23.0 miles). Here in 1855 the Mormon Church directed the founding of the Elk Mountain Mission in an attempt to expand its realm. When Ute Indians attacked them that same year, the Mormons abandoned the mission. Resettlement in the 1870s proved permanent, and Moab developed into a supply point for the region. Successive uranium and tourist booms have since driven the local economy.

Continue north and cross the Colorado River at 3.0 miles. North of Moab, the Spanish Trail followed Courthouse Wash up Moab Canyon. On the Spanish Trail, near the junction of the Dead Horse Point road (SR 313) and US 191, you will see the landscape of Arches National Park in the distance on your right.

Continue north to CRESCENT JUNCTION (31.5 miles). The Spanish Trail angled northwest across the Green River Desert on your left, parallel to the power lines, through the Green River missile facility, and on to the Green River Crossing, north of the town of Green River.

At Crescent Junction, travel west on I-70 to the town of GREEN RIVER (19.0 miles). Visit the John Wesley Powell River History Museum in Green River.

Starting in the Wind River Mountains of Wyoming, the Green River flows through southwest Wyoming, enters northeast Utah, passes through Dinosaur National Monument on the Utah-Colorado border, and then travels south until its junction with the Colorado River in Canyonlands National Park. A small party led by Major John Wesley Powell in 1869 was the first to travel through the system of intricate canyons along the Green and Colorado rivers.

GREEN RIVER, UTAH TO SALINA, UTAH

Tempting as it must have been to remain at the crossroads oasis of Green River, Spanish Trail travelers pushed on over dry, open terrain toward the formidable San Rafael Swell, a deeply eroded, oval-shaped upheaval in the earth's crust. Piercing an enormous, jagged, inclined ridge (San Rafael Reef), today's I-70 bisects the geologic uplift, offering captivating views of an intricate landscape of sedimentary rock. Much of this uninhabited region, seventy miles long by thirty miles wide, remains remote and impassable.

Place names within the San Rafael Swell, such as Horse Thief Trail and Secret Mesa, suggest that the area gave sanctuary to outlaws. Indeed, in the post-Spanish Trail days, Butch Cassidy and other members of the infamous Wild Bunch found escape routes through the labyrinth of rock. Lawmen were generally unwilling to chase bandits into the wild, almost frightening, array of canyons and sandstone formations.

Leaving the Green River Crossing, Gunnison's party in 1853 moved southwest over the Spanish Trail to Saleratus Wash, then ascended its course as it looped to the northwest. The explorers forged ahead to Green River Spring, known today as TRAIL SPRING (125.8 miles), approximately 13.0 miles from the river ford. According to Gunnison, the Ute Indians referred to the waterhole within the San Rafael Swell as Akanaquint Spring. Today the spring is overrun by tamarisk and is used as a stock-watering pond.

Hoofs sank deep into the sandy wash beyond Green River Spring as pack animals struggled north up the dim trail to reach Lost Spring Wash. Here, at 128.8 miles, Gunnison left the Spanish Trail, and circled north around the difficult interior of the Swell.

The trail proceeded into the San Rafael Swell, negotiating the sands of Lost Spring Wash. It emerged from the wash at CEMENT CROSSING (139.0 miles), on the unused grade of the Denver and Rio Grande Railroad. (After engineering a fifty-mile railroad bed that cut across the northern part of the Swell in 1882, the D&RG canceled the project in favor of a direct route from Green River to Price, Utah. Sections of the abandoned grade closely parallel the Spanish Trail.) From Cement Crossing, the trail makes its way along Big Hole Wash toward the BIG HOLES (142.3 miles), in Packsaddle Gulch. Throughout this reach and beyond, we are guided by the accounts of the Mormon Elk Mountain Mission group, which followed the Spanish Trail in 1855 on its way to colonize Moab. At Big Holes, the Mormon party found natural tanks carved into exposed bedrock, which supplied them with ample water.

Beyond Big Holes, the trail emerged into the open area passing between the broken rim of the San Rafael River drainage — gashed by canyons — on the left and the thousand-foot-high cliffs of Cedar Mountain on the right.

The trail continued a west-northwest course to LITTLE HOLES (151.8 miles), 9.5 miles from Big Holes, where water was found in natural

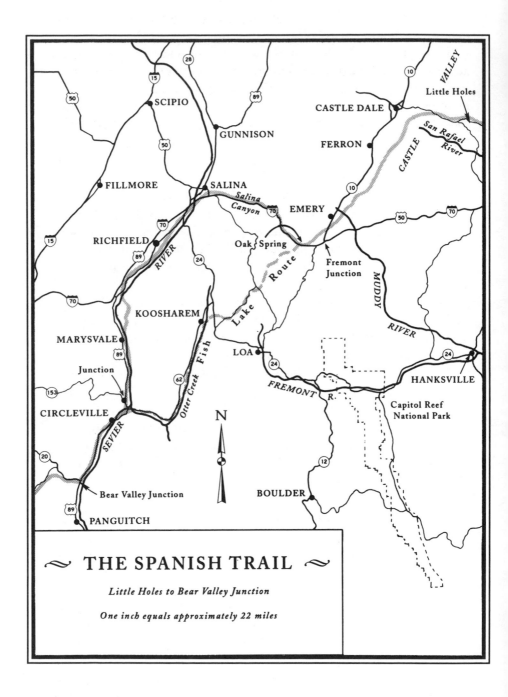

~ **THE SPANISH TRAIL** ~

Little Holes to Bear Valley Junction

One inch equals approximately 22 miles

rock reservoirs, though it was nearly inaccessible to travelers. The difficulties of getting water here are described by Oliver B. Huntington, diarist for the 1855 Elk Mountain Mission, who says: "[We] clambered down to an overhanging rock and drawed up water with lassos and then passed it from hand to hand until it reached the top. This was very dangerous work, occupied ten men. A little after dark all the stock had got a taste of water and very few all they wanted." Huntington's description of Little Holes is accurate. But in a good water year, animals in some numbers could have been driven to ample pools of water at the head of the gulch.

From Little Holes, the Spanish Trail advanced westward, threading its way through FURNITURE DRAW (153.8 miles), then carved a trace along the expanse of Buckhorn Flat leading to the Black Hills. The trail left the San Rafael Swell, ascending the Black Hills at the base of Little Cedar Mountain. It cut a path up the low, gravelly slope on the east side of the Black Hills before dropping into Castle Valley. At the Black Hills, the trail reached its NORTHERNMOST POINT (164.3 miles) — approximately 39°12' north latitude.

From here, the well-marked trail carried early travelers on a southwesterly course along the wide open floor of Castle Valley. After detouring around the rugged canyons of the San Rafael Swell in October of 1853, the Gunnison party returned to the well-worn trail in Castle Valley. Lieutenant E. G. Beckwith, second in command of the Gunnison expedition, described the trail where the party rejoined it: "The Spanish trail, though but seldom used of late years, is still very distinct where the soil washes but slightly. On some such spaces to-day we counted from fourteen to twenty parallel trails, of the ordinary size of Indian trails or horse-paths, on a way of barely fifty feet in width."

Continuing along the trail, the Gunnison party drank from the "abundance of cool water" at OAK SPRING (207.5 miles), south of Castle Valley. Near the present Oak Spring Ranch, the expedition turned up Ivie Creek to the summit of the Wasatch Plateau. I-70 has obliterated the Spanish Trail along this stretch of canyon. High on a canyon wall alongside the trail, however, is a dramatic Indian pictograph that Gunnison saw in 1853, of which the 1855 Huntington expedition left a detailed description.

In the canyon, where RED CREEK (211.3 miles) empties into Ivie Creek, the Spanish Trail branches. The southern branch crossed Fish Lake Plateau via Johnson Reservoir and Fish Lake. It rejoined the northern branch, or main trail, near the town of Junction, at the confluence of the Sevier River with its East Fork. Kit Carson and George D. Brewerton popularized the route in 1848. The Fish Lake Route, a distance of seventy-two miles, saved travelers more than twenty miles, but they encountered elevations in excess of nine thousand feet.

The main Spanish Trail continued across the Wasatch Plateau by way of 7,800-foot WASATCH PASS (213.8 miles), the dividing line between the drainage of the Colorado River and the Great Basin. Below the pass, I-70 unites with the trail as it twists through Salina Canyon to the SALT DEPOSITS (238.0 miles), near the foot of the canyon. In 1853 the Edward F. Beale railroad survey party observed these "mines of rock-salt," and claimed that the Rio Salado (Salina Creek/Meadow Creek) derived its name from them.

The automobile tour starts at the JOHN WESLEY POWELL RIVER HISTORY MUSEUM in the town of Green River. Green River is located in east-central Utah, 182 miles from Salt Lake City.

You will be traveling on the Green River Cutoff, an unimproved road north of I-70, which parallels the Spanish Trail.

Optional route to Fremont Junction. If you wish to avoid the Green River Cutoff, you can proceed west on I-70 to the junction with SR 10. Spectacular views of the San Rafael Reef and the eroded canyons of the San Rafael Swell can be seen from I-70. Robbers' Roost, hideout of outlaw Butch Cassidy and his gang, is located south of I-70. It is approximately 72.0 miles from Green River to Fremont Junction via I-70.

From the museum, travel west on I-70 to the US 6/191 EXIT (5.0 miles).

Travel north on US 6/191 to the junction with the unmarked GREEN RIVER CUTOFF (17.0 miles), an unimproved road on the left. Turn left onto the Green River Cutoff and travel west. You will drive under the old D&RG (now Southern Pacific) railroad overpass. *Caution: the Green River Cutoff should be used only in dry weather.*

At 24.5 miles, the Little Holes are located south of the road. At 26.6 miles is the junction of the Spanish Trail with the Green River Cutoff in Furniture Draw, and at 39.4 miles is the junction with Huntington Creek. Continue west to the JUNCTION (44.0 miles) with SR 10, 1.0 miles north of Castle Dale.

Travel south on SR 10 to Castle Dale, and continue south through the towns of Clawson, Ferron, and Emery to FREMONT JUNCTION (approximately 40.0 miles), the junction of I-70 and SR 10.

Travel west on I-70 to MILEPOST 55 (32.8 miles), near the mouth of Salina Canyon. Look for the salt deposits in a side canyon, north of I-70.

Continue west to the town of SALINA (2.0 miles). Salina is named for the salt deposits in the area. Originally settled in 1866, Salina was vacated because of Indian troubles, and permanently settled in 1871.

SALINA, UTAH TO CEDAR CITY, UTAH

Below the canyon, near the mouth of Salina Creek, the Spanish Trail forded the SEVIER RIVER (243.0 miles), or Rio Severo, and followed the stream southward along its west bank. Passing through the rich pasturage of Sevier River Valley in 1853, Gwinn Harris Heap of the Beale expedition wrote that it "surpassed in beauty and fertility anything we had yet seen." He had noted earlier, "the grass was of the most luxuriant description, and reached above our saddle girths."

The trail meandered upstream, past the present towns of Richfield and Elsinore, and continued to a point near the mouth of CLEAR CREEK (274.0 miles). Avoiding the narrow Marysvale Canyon, early travelers "passed over a steep hill" east of US 89 — climbing a ridge one thousand feet above the Sevier River — and descended into the next valley.

Near the town of Marysvale, trail riders returned to the SEVIER RIVER (286.5 miles), and ascended it to its junction with the EAST FORK (305.5 miles) of the Sevier. Here the southern branch of the Spanish Trail, or Fish Lake Route, joined the main trail. When the Beale expedition reached this point in 1853, they found the Fish Lake route "long disused" and "almost obliterated." Today, US 89 closely parallels the route of the main trail as it continues upstream along the Sevier River, passing through the pastoral settings in Circle Valley.

South of Circleville Canyon, the trail reached BEAR VALLEY JUNCTION (325.5 miles), where it left the Sevier River and swung to the west up Bear Creek. SR 20 follows the course of the trail westward as it steadily climbs the canyon. Where a valley opens out in the mountain landscape, the Spanish Trail turned abruptly to the southwest. It continued up Bear Creek along a natural route through Lower and Upper Bear valleys. Then it crossed a divide, and moved down Little Creek.

Descending the rugged, narrow defile of Little Creek on the Markagunt Plateau, the Spanish Trail penetrated the Hurricane Cliffs to enter Parowan Valley near the town of PARAGONAH (352.0 miles). Here the trail made its dramatic entrance into the basin of Little Salt Lake on the southern extremity of Utah's Great Basin. On 1 October 1848, Orville C. Pratt traveled "up the steepest of hills, then down places which it would seem almost impossible to descend. again in deep and precipitous canions: until at length *suddenly broke upon us* one of the finest and most extensive valleys I have seen in the whole western country!" (Emphasis added.) Four years earlier, John C. Frémont passed through the same valley and recorded that Little Salt Lake lies "nearly opposite a gap in the chain of mountains through which the Spanish Trail passes."

Mormon diaries give us additional insight into the location and character of the trail, and trailside features, throughout southwestern Utah and beyond. Addison Pratt, a Mormon missionary bound for the South Seas who accompanied the Jefferson Hunt wagon train to California in 1849, made the following observation of Parowan Valley:

> This is a large valley and affords lots of grass but there is not enough water to accommodate a large settlement. The lake is about 12 miles long and the water appears to be more impregnated with saleratus than salt. There are plenty of wild geese and ducks about it and in the bottom is plenty of hares and sage hens. The mountains on the east side are very high and well timbered with cedar and pine.

From the east side of Parowan Valley, the Spanish Trail carried California-bound travelers on a level path to the site of the once-abundant springs at ENOCH (368.0 miles). The trail, which followed a southwesterly path past Little Salt Lake, is now paralleled by I-15. It swung around the southern end of the hills west of Parowan Valley to reach Ojo de San Jose, or San Jose Spring. On Frémont's map of his second expedition, it is labeled St. Joseph's Spring. This vital water source was "one of the finest fountains and streams of water on the entire route," noted Orville Pratt. Here, northeast of Cedar City, Mormons established the settlement of Elkhorn Springs in 1851, known today as Enoch.

The automobile tour starts at the JUNCTION of I-70 and the town of Salina. Salina is located in south-central Utah, 142 miles from Salt Lake City.

Travel west on I-70 to EXIT 23 (32.0 miles), "Sevier Junction."

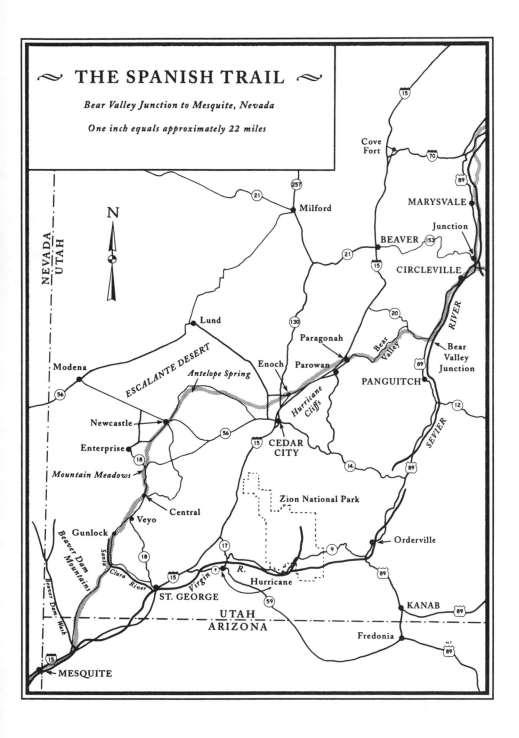

~ **THE SPANISH TRAIL** ~

Bear Valley Junction to Mesquite, Nevada

One inch equals approximately 22 miles

Travel south on US 89 to the JUNCTION (30.0 miles) with SR 62, near the town of Junction. Here is where the Fish Lake Route, or southern branch, of the Spanish Trail joined the main Spanish Trail. Along US 89 you will find Big Rock Candy Mountain, a tourist stop between the towns of Monroe and Marysville. Old Spanish Trail signs at Marysville and Junction commemorate the route.

Continue south to CIRCLEVILLE (6.0 miles). Approximately 3.0 miles south of Circleville is a log cabin located along US 89 on the right — the boyhood home of Robert LeRoy Parker, more familiarly known in outlaw annals as Butch Cassidy of Wild Bunch notoriety. A descendent of Utah Mormon pioneers, Parker took the name Cassidy in his late teens as he began to stray into a life of banditry. There are conflicting versions of his last days. Popular lore had him die with his partner Harry Longabaugh (the Sundance Kid) in a gunfight with Bolivian soldiers; but the prevailing opinion argues that both he and Longabaugh turned up later in the United States. Cassidy died — depending on who tells it — in 1937 after a business career in the Pacific Northwest; or in relative seclusion under an assumed name in either Utah, Nevada, or Wyoming as a law-abiding citizen. He remains, however, among the most colorful figures in Utah history and the mystery of how he died contributes to his mythical stature.

Continue south to the JUNCTION (17.0 miles) with SR 20, known as Bear Valley Junction, or Orton.

Travel west on SR 20, which parallels the Spanish Trail up Bear Creek. At 6.5 miles the Spanish Trail turns southwest through Lower Bear Valley and Upper Bear Valley and down Little Creek Canyon. Continue to the JUNCTION (20.5 miles) with I-15.

Travel south on I-15 to PARAGONAH (13.0 miles). Near Milepost 83 you can see Little Creek Canyon in the distance on your left. This is where the Spanish Trail enters Parowan Valley. At 1.5 miles south of Exit 78 ("Parowan") you can see a faint view of the dry playa of Little Salt Lake at the base of the hills to your right.

Continue south to ENOCH (19.0 miles). Here the Spanish Trail leaves I-15 as it makes its way to Pinto Creek at Newcastle, via Iron Springs and Antelope Spring.

Continue south to the JUNCTION (11.0 miles) with SR 56.

Travel east on SR 56 to Cedar City.

CEDAR CITY, UTAH TO UTAH-ARIZONA BORDER

From Enoch, the trail followed a west-southwesterly course over the open country of Cedar Valley to the gap between Granite Mountain and The Three Peaks. Where the trail approached the gap, travelers halted at a location that trail-researcher S. Alva Matheson of Cedar City has labeled IRON SPRINGS CAMP (377.0 miles). Beyond the campsite, the trail reached Iron Springs, paralleling the present route of the Union Pacific Railroad. Dr. Thomas Flint who traveled this portion of the trail on 19 October 1853, observed: "Drove to Iron Springs and creek where we camped. Boulders of Magnetic Iron ore laying around in abundance."

The Spanish Trail followed Iron Springs Creek in a northwesterly direction, extending into the southern fringe of the Escalante Desert. It continued westward over the flat, open desert to ANTELOPE SPRING (391.3 miles), at the northern base of the Antelope Range. The distance from Iron Springs to Antelope Spring closely fits the mileage indicated by Addison Pratt on 2 November 1849. Leaving Iron Springs, his party "travelled 11 miles and camped at a spring on the mountain side. The spring oozes out of the ground and makes a large stream which, after running a few rods, sinks back into the ground." Dr. Thomas Flint traveled over the same barren road from Iron Springs on 20 October 1853, and described the area: "No feed, but sagebrush. Came to a spring in the side of the mountain, scarcely enough water for our use. Some scattering of bunch grass on the foot of the mountain. A kind of valley without water."

From Antelope Spring, the trail swung around the northern base of the Antelope Range, then pursued a southwesterly course to PINTO CREEK (402.0 miles), near the present town of Newcastle. Throughout the distance from Enoch to Newcastle, on the main line to California, we can rely on John C. Frémont's map to further pinpoint the Spanish Trail. Although no place names are given along this stretch, his map shows the route as described above. His table of distances supplies further evidence of the trail's course to Pinto Creek and beyond.

Historians LeRoy and Ann Hafen claim that the term Pinto was most likely a "misinterpretation of the spelling of Piute," the name which Addison Pratt applied to the creek in 1849. Pratt was a member of the Jefferson Hunt wagon train, a party of forty-niners who decided, beyond Pinto Creek, to part ways. Anxious to get to the California gold fields, several members of the party ventured from the proven trail. Their wanderings through the desert led them into Death Valley, where they struck misfortune and gave the valley its name. Near the Spanish Trail, about 6.0 miles from Pinto Creek, a stone monument to Jefferson Hunt and the Spanish Trail reminds passersby of this fateful departure from the well-established corridor to California.

The main trail to California follows the deeply eroded Meadow Creek southward up Holt Canyon through the faint traces of the early farming village of Holt, established in post-trail days. The old trail crests a low divide and continues south to MOUNTAIN MEADOWS (417.0 miles), a valley of plentiful grass and water four to five miles long, with an elevation of about 5,900 feet. At Mountain Meadows, travelers passed over the rim of the Great Basin into the water drainage of the Virgin River, a tributary of the Colorado River.

Here modern travelers arrive at a scene of dramatic misfortune. The history of the meadows has long been associated with the infamous Mountain Meadows Massacre, where, in 1857, for multiple reasons, some Mormons and Indians massacred a train of emigrants coming from Missouri and Arkansas. Public perception of Mountain Meadows has been altered by the tragedy that occurred here.

If we take our focus off the massacre, we get a clearer picture of this rich meadowland on the rim of the Great Basin. Known as "las Vegas de Santa Clara," it was an important resting and recruiting place for traveling companies on the Spanish Trail. John C. Frémont, whose party arrived here on 12 May 1844, after an exhaustive desert march, found "the terminating point of the desert . . . where the annual caravan from California to New Mexico halted and recruited for some weeks. It was a very suitable place to recover from the fatigue and exhaustion of a month's suffering in the hot and sterile desert." Frémont described the site as "an extensive mountain meadow, rich in bunch grass, and fresh with numerous springs of clear water, all refreshing and delightful to look upon."

In addition to Frémont's account, we have glowing reports by other parties: Orville C. Pratt, who "camped at the Vegas of Santa Clara" to recruit his animals on 4–5 October 1848, wrote: "The animals are doing finely on the excellent grass they get here. There is fine & tender grass enough growing on this Vegas to fatten a thousand head of horses or cattle." George D. Brewerton, who accompanied Kit Carson in 1848 on his journey over the Spanish Trail, gives us this description of Mountain Meadows: "The noise of running water, the large grassy meadows, from which the spot takes its name, and the green hills which circle it round

— all tend to captivate the eye and please the senses of the way-worn voyageur."

In his reminiscent account of travels over the Spanish Trail, Anthony W. Ivins described Mountain Meadows as "a small valley in the tops of the mountains, where springs spread over the surface and formed one of those beauty spots, found only in mountain landscapes. Since the days of the pioneers, heavy floods have cut a deep gully through the valley, which has drained the water from the surface, the grass has disappeared, and sagebrush taken its place."

The deep gully that cuts through the center of the meadows is the eroded bed of Magotsu Creek, a tributary of the Santa Clara River. It illustrates the erosion that occurs when trails are developed in the soft soil of a desert environment.

The trail landscape beyond Mountain Meadows is richly diverse. The altered appearance of the meadows contrasts sharply with an original section of the Spanish Trail that can still be seen on the slope to the south. Below the meadows, the trail descends two miles along a primitive path to Kane Spring, where overland travelers watered their animals before proceeding down the adjoining wash. Along the channel below the spring, early travelers resumed a course over "a rough, rocky, moun-tainous road," now paralleled by SR 18, to present-day Central. Those who traverse this length of highway are able to enjoy the view of the Pine Valley Mountain peaks to the east. Observing the peaks on his 1844 trek over the Spanish Trail, John C. Frémont noted: They "showed out hand-somely — high and rugged with precipices, and covered with snow for about two thousand feet from their summits down."

Below Central, travelers on the Spanish Trail veered southwest, within sight of the volcanic formations in the area (including the Veyo volcano), to reach the lower length of MAGOTSU CREEK (427.5 miles), then followed that stream to its junction with Moody Wash near today's old Biglow Ranch. Early trail riders continued down MOODY WASH (431.5 miles), to the Santa Clara River, a tributary of the Virgin River, which is labeled on Frémont's map.

The history of the Spanish Trail is as varied as its landscape. Along the Santa Clara River we find the pioneer Mormon village of GUN-LOCK (437.0 miles), established in 1857. Gunlock was an offshoot of an earlier settlement founded downstream, a short distance from the Span-ish Trail, at Santa Clara. Frontier scout Jacob Hamblin and others estab-lished a Mormon mission among the Southern Paiutes at Santa Clara in

1854. The Paiutes who inhabited, and still inhabit, the area, comprised one of the larger Indian populations on the Spanish Trail. It was important to keep peaceful relations with the Indians living along the route that Mormons regarded as an essential corridor to California. Hamblin played a major role in befriending the Indians and in helping colonize the Santa Clara River area in the 1850s. The Indian mission at Santa Clara proved very successful. Thereafter, Mormon colonizing efforts expanded into the region, where in 1861 they founded St. George in the center of Utah's Dixie.

The Spanish Trail, as it ran through southwestern Utah and beyond, passed through the Southern Paiute homelands. Related linguistically to the Utes, the Paiutes lived in small encampments and journeyed about hunting and gathering, making skillful use of the shifting resources in a desert environment. Along the Santa Clara River, they developed farms, which Orville C. Pratt in 1848 identified as the "Piute Cornfields." Modern explorers can still find patches of sweet, yellow corn being cultivated along the stream.

In early times, passing caravans and wagon trains that followed the Spanish Trail trampled the farmlands of the Paiutes and denuded the desert landscape. In addition, Paiutes suffered regular abuse by slave catchers and traders who seized their women and children and sold them as servants or slaves in the settlements of California and New Mexico. Paiutes were not horse breeders and had difficulty defending themselves against mounted parties, including the Utes, who often raided their encampments, taking captives. New Mexican traders also played a major role in Indian slave trafficking among the Paiutes, as a subordinate line of business. Pack trains regularly victimized Paiutes, who began to retaliate in later trail years.

Some of the tormented Paiutes fought back, but many of them retreated from their homelands near the Santa Clara River out of fear of slave catchers. Traveling along the river in 1853, Gwinn Harris Heap of the Beale Survey observed that the Indians were fearful that his party might be slavers. He reported that a woman hid her child in a wicker basket, and when one of the party looked into the basket, he saw "a little naked fellow, his teeth chattering with fear."

For nine miles the trail advances over broken ground, shaded by cottonwoods, along the bed and banks of the Santa Clara River which runs, as Solomon Carvalho wrote in May 1854, "in a serpentine direction, almost due south." The trail crosses the river a number of times before leaving it at a point on the Shivwits (Paiute) Indian Reservation where the stream makes a broad bend to the east.

In addition to the impact of Indians on its history, the Spanish Trail, from its beginning, has been a theater for human experience. Faint reminders of nineteenth-century human passage through the Santa Clara River area are still evident. One mile from the river, trail riders reached CAMP SPRING (444.8 miles), a water hole which played a greater role in post-trail days. Chiseled on the rocks nearby is a pioneer register dating back to the mid-1800s. Research in government documents reveals the history behind some of the inscriptions.

In 1864, Colonel Patrick Edward Connor, commander of Camp Douglas in Salt Lake City, ordered a military force led by Captain George F. Price, Company M, 2nd Cavalry, to establish a military wagon road to the upper point of navigation on the Colorado River. The expedition made its way to Mountain Meadows, where the soldiers built a memorial to the families who were slain in the Mountain Meadows Massacre. A few days later, the troops advanced down the Santa Clara River and stopped at Camp Spring. Here some of the soldiers left their names and recorded their military attachment in the nearby hills.

Leaving Camp Spring, the expedition followed the Spanish Trail to Las Vegas, where they turned south; after a grueling journey, they reached Fort Mohave on the Colorado. Captain Price then issued a report declaring the expedition a success and recommending that further explorations be made.

Those who explore traces of the Spanish Trail beyond Camp Spring will note that it climbs a steep grade crossing the Beaver Dam Mountains, followed today by old US 91. At the summit, the trail approaches an elevation over 4,700 feet, then starts down a gently sloping desert terrain. Today's unmarked highway closely approximates the trail as it winds its way through a forest of Joshua trees to the UTAH-ARIZONA BORDER (460.0 miles).

Beyond the border, the Spanish Trail cuts through northwestern Arizona and follows the Virgin River to Mormon Mesa. It crosses the mesa in southern Nevada, and probes the desert country to the west, to reach the historic oasis at Las Vegas. The trail then continues over the Mojave Desert, descends Cajon Pass, and moves on to the plaza in Los Angeles, completing its splendid passage to the coastal settlements of the Pacific.

The automobile tour starts at the JUNCTION of I-15 and SR 56, west of the town of Cedar City. Cedar City is located in southwestern Utah, 250 miles from Salt Lake City.

Travel west on SR 56. At approximately 3.5 miles you will find an Escalante Trail marker on your right. Look for the Spanish Trail marker on your left just before you enter NEWCASTLE (30.0 miles).

From Newcastle, travel southwest along a graded road to the JUNCTION (8.0 miles) with SR 18.

Optional tour to the Jefferson Hunt/Spanish Trail Monument. Approximately 5.0 miles from Newcastle is a junction with a road heading south. Turn onto this road and travel 0.5 miles to the JEFFERSON HUNT/ SPANISH TRAIL MONUMENT.
Return to the graded road between Newcastle and SR 18.

One mile east of SR 18 is a jeep trail, known locally as Meadow Canyon Road, that runs parallel to the Spanish Trail southward to the lower end of Mountain Meadows. Travel south on SR 18 to the MOUNTAIN MEADOWS AREA (13.0 miles). Visit the monument at the Mountain Meadows Massacre site.

Continue south through the towns of Central and VEYO (11.0 miles).

In Veyo, follow Center Street, the road running westward from the center of Veyo. Note the Veyo volcano south of town. Continue south on Center Street (old US 91) to GUNLOCK (8.0 miles). The unmarked road from Veyo to Shivwits via Gunlock is known locally as the Gunlock Road.

Continue south to SHIVWITS (9.0 miles). The road runs parallel to the Spanish Trail past the town of Gunlock and Gunlock Reservoir, and down the Santa Clara River. The road leaves the Spanish Trail where the pavement turns eastward.

Continue southwest to the UTAH-ARIZONA BORDER (16.0 miles). The road runs along the Spanish Trail to the summit of the Beaver Dam Mountains. Below the summit, to the south, the road parallels the Spanish Trail to Beaver Dam, Arizona.

Continue south to the JUNCTION (8.0 miles) with I-15. At this point you are 323 miles southwest of Salt Lake City and 89 miles east of Las Vegas, Nevada.

The Bidwell-Bartleson Trail

Roy D. Tea

Oneida Narrows, formed by the Bear River as it cuts through the mountains. *Photograph by Roy D. Tea*

HISTORICAL PERSPECTIVE

Prior to the year 1841, only a few emigrants had made the westward journey overland to Oregon and California. The formation of the Western Emigration Society in 1841, however, permanently changed this situation. Organized in western Missouri to help overland emigrants prepare for the journey westward, the Western Emigration Society influenced the large migration that followed in the 1840s.

John Bidwell had migrated to western Missouri from New York in search of adventure, and his ambitions coincided with the aims of the Western Emigration Society. After meeting mountain man Antoine Robidoux, who painted an attractive picture of California, Bidwell was determined to head westward to California. The party that he traveled with was the first planned overland company to emigrate to California.

The emigrant company was organized on 18 May 1841 with John Bartleson elected as captain. Bartleson would not go with the company unless he was made captain. They were almost completely ignorant of the route west to California, but, fortunately, they were able to travel to the Rocky Mountains with a party of Jesuit missionaries guided by Thomas F. "Broken Hand" Fitzpatrick. From Soda Springs, Idaho, to their destination in California, they were left to their own resources. Having been advised by Fitzpatrick to travel south of the Snake River drainage and north of Great Salt Lake, they entered present-day Utah and became the first emigrants with wagons to travel across northern Utah.

They abandoned their wagons in eastern Nevada and continued on to California. With a little better reconnoitering to the west of Lucin, Utah, a trail could have been blazed to the head of the Humboldt River near Wells, Nevada, along the present alignment of the Southern Pacific Railroad. The route traveled by the Bidwell-Bartleson party across Utah could have become the California Trail instead of the trail later established through the City of Rocks, Granite Pass, and Goose Creek, north of Wells, Nevada.

Five years later, the Bryant-Russell party encountered evidence of the Bidwell-Bartleson party ten miles southwest of Donner Spring. No other reference is made to the 1841 trail, even though the Harlan-Young, Hoppe-Lienhard, and Donner-Reed parties also traveled a portion of the trail into Nevada in 1846. In later years, wagon trains traveled across Park Valley, following close to the railroad after it was built in 1869. These wagon trains probably traveled some sections of the Bidwell-Bartleson trail.

This chapter covers that portion of the Bidwell-Bartleson trail from Soda Springs, Idaho, south along the Bear River to Great Salt Lake, west and south past Donner Spring, south around Pilot Peak, and west through Silver Zone Pass into Nevada. Because of the length of the trail, the tour is divided into two parts: Soda Springs, Idaho to Corinne, Utah and Corinne, Utah to Wendover, Utah.

The tour includes excerpts from Bidwell's diary and from the diary of James John, another party member. Following his arrival in California, Bidwell's diary was carried to the eastern states and published in 1842. It was read and carried by westward travelers, becoming the first overland emigrant "guide." The diary of James John was not discovered until the twentieth century, and was published first in 1991 in Doyce Nunis's book *The Bidwell-Bartleson Party: 1841 California Emigrant Adventure,* along with the Bidwell diary and other documents relating to the emigrant party. The two diaries complement each other.

SODA SPRINGS, IDAHO TO CORINNE, UTAH

The automobile tour starts at the JUNCTION of Main Street and US 30 in Soda Springs, Idaho. Soda Springs is located in southeastern Idaho, 165 miles north of Salt Lake City.

Located on the Oregon Trail, Soda Springs has been known since pioneer days for its mineral salt springs, one of which was named Beer Spring. Alexander Reservoir now covers most of these springs. Writing in his journal on 10 August 1841, John Bidwell described the springs:

> The day was fine and pleasant; a soft and cheerful breeze and the sky bedimmed by smoke brought to mind the tranquil season of Autumn. A distance of 10 miles took us to the Soda Fountain, where we stopped the remainder of the day. This is a noted place in the mountains and is considered a great curiosity — within the circumference of 3 or 4 miles there are included no less than 100 springs, some bursting out on top of the ground, others along the banks of the river. The water is strongly impregnated with Soda, and wherever it gushes out of the ground, a sediment is deposited, of redish color, which petrifies and forms around the springs large mounds of porous rock; some of which are no less than fifty feet high — some of these fountains have become entirely dry, in consequence of the column of water which they contained, becoming so high, as to create sufficient power by its pressure, to force the water to the surface in another place, in several of the springs the water was lukewarm — but none were

very cold — The ground was very dry at this time, and made a noise as we passed over it with horses, as though it was hollow underneath. Cedar grows here in abundance, and the scenery of the country is romantic. Father De Smet, with 2 or 3 flat head Indians, started about dark this evening to go to Fort Hall which was about 50 miles distance.

Travel west on US 30. At 1.2 miles are two historical signs on the left that explain about Soda Springs and Colonel Patrick Edward Connor. Continue west to OREGON TRAIL STATE PARK (2.7 miles).

Optional tour to Oregon Trail State Park. Enter Oregon Trail State Park and note the trail ruts on the right and left of the road.
Return to US 30.

Continue west to the JUNCTION (2.5 miles) with a road on the left, next to an Idaho highway maintenance station. By this station are two historical signs: one sign describes the separation of the Bidwell–Bartleson party, and the other sign describes the volcanic eruptions which changed the course of the Bear River 28,000 years ago.

Optional tour to the Bear River overlook. Turn left onto the road by the Idaho highway maintenance station. Travel south 0.5 miles to a concrete dam on the Bear River. Note the channel depth of the Bear River as it flows west and then south.
Return to US 30.

The Bear River heads in Utah's Summit County in the Uinta Mountains, flows through Wyoming's Uinta County, Idaho's Bear Lake, Caribou and Franklin counties, and Utah's Cache and Box Elder counties along a meandering 350-mile course to empty into Great Salt Lake at Bear River Migratory Bird Refuge, 90 miles from its source. The Bear River is the largest river located entirely inside the Great Basin, its flow being exceeded only by the Green and Colorado rivers. At intervals along its course, dams impound and divert the waters for industrial and agricultural purposes.

Michael Bourdon, a twenty-one-year-old French Canadian fur trapper of the Hudson's Bay Company, is given credit for naming the Bear River in 1818 while trapping in the area. He was killed by Indians there the following year. The Indians had names for the river — "Quee-yah-pah" for Tobacco Root Water, and "Gull-yah-pah" for Tobacco Water. These names refer to the color of the river in its lower reaches. The name

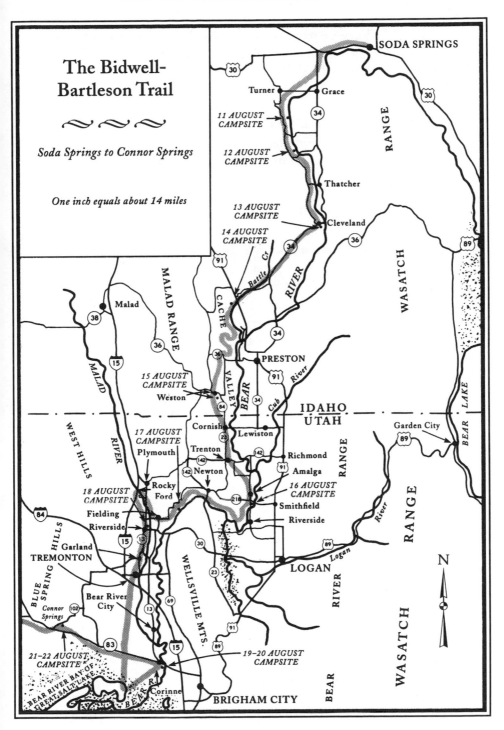

The Bidwell-
Bartleson Trail

Soda Springs to Connor Springs

One inch equals about 14 miles

Michael Bourdon gave refers to the numerous black, brown, and grizzly bears found in the region at that time.

Continue west to the JUNCTION (1.0 miles) with a gravel road on the left.

Optional tour to pioneer burial site. This road is rough and is not recommended for passenger cars. Travel south on this gravel road 0.5 miles to a fenced area where fifteen unknown pioneers are buried. *Return to US 30.*

Continue west to the JUNCTION (0.9 miles) with SR 34.

Optional tour to Oregon Trail ruts. Turn right onto old US 30. At 0.2 miles turn right, and continue east 0.5 miles to the mounds of dirt that block the road. On the left a fence ends. Park and walk past this fence about three hundred feet to view the Oregon Trail ruts in the sagebrush near the railroad fence. This is west of the location where the Bidwell-Bartleson party and the De Smet party separated, the Bidwell-Bartleson party going south and the De Smet party going northwest. John Bidwell described this separation:

> Having traveled about 6 miles this morning the Company came to a halt — the Oregon Company were now going to leave Bear river for Ft. Hall, which is situated on Lewis River, a branch of the Columbia — many, who purposed in setting out, to go immediately through to the California, here, concluded to go into Oregon so that the California company now consisted of only 32 men and one woman and child, there being but one family. The two companies, after bidding each other a parting farewell, started and were soon out of sight, several of our company however went to Ft. Hall to procure provisions, and to hire if possible a pilot to conduct us to the gap in the California Mountains, or a least, to the head of Mary's river, we were therefore to move on slowly till their return. Encamped on Bear river, having come about 12 miles.

Return to the junction of US 30 and SR 34.

Travel south on SR 34 to the town of GRACE (5.0 miles). Turn right onto Center Street.

Travel west on Center Street. At 1.5 miles cross the Black Canyon of the Bear, where the Bear River has cut a deep channel through the black volcanic rock. This channel becomes deeper downstream as the Bear River cuts through the end of the volcanic rock and flows into the valley.

Continue west to the JUNCTION (3.0 miles) with the Hegstrom road.

Turn left onto the Hegstrom road, continue to a bend in the road, then turn right and continue to the JUNCTION (2.0 miles) with Gentile Valley road.

Travel south on Gentile Valley road to the JUNCTION (1.9 miles) with Ralph Hanson road.

Optional tour to 11 August campsite. Travel east then south on Ralph Hanson Road, and at 0.9 miles stop on top of a hill, about four hundred feet from a house at the end of the lane. This is the 11 AUGUST CAMPSITE of the Bidwell-Bartleson party. Look west to the mountain and its two peaks and you will see where John Bidwell and James John saw snow on 11 August. John Bidwell described the scene:

> I, in company with another man [J. John], went some distance below the camp to fish in the river; fished sometime without success — concluded we could spend the afternoon more agreeably, the day was uncomfortably warm, could find no copses of willows these we did not like to enter on account of the danger of falling in with bears, we concluded to ascend the mountain, where, were two spots of snow in full view, in order to enjoy the contrast between a scorching valley, and a snowy mountain.

After midnight, Bidwell and John found a place to sleep under a stunted fir tree. In the morning, they discovered quantities of shaggy hair. This had been the lair of grizzly bears. They reached the snow that morning, and, after putting some in a handkerchief, they hurried down the mountain back to camp where they were chastised by Bartleson and greeted with joy by the rest of the party.

Return to Gentile Valley road.

Continue south to the JUNCTION (3.2 miles) with Thatcher road and the 12 AUGUST CAMPSITE. Turn right onto Thatcher road, and travel south past the Mormon Church's Thatcher wardhouse to the JUNCTION (7.2 miles) with Cleveland road. Travel south on Cleveland road to the JUNCTION (6.0 miles) with 13400 North. Turn left and travel east on 13400 North to the JUNCTION (0.7 miles) with SR 34. At this point, you can see the Oneida Narrows to the south. The Oneida Narrows is where the Bear River cuts though the mountains and where, downstream, a dam has been built to form Oneida Narrows Reservoir.

The 13 AUGUST CAMPSITE was on the river by the narrows. James John described the campsite: "This morning we passed by a hot spring near the encampment it is constantly boiling and smoking and is strongly impregnated with soda. We traveled about 15 miles today over hills and mountains and encamped on a small brook about 4 miles from the river." This hot spring can be seen on the south side of US 34, just after entering the highway.

Travel southwest on SR 34, paralleling the Bidwell-Bartleson route, to the JUNCTION (11.0 miles) with Mail Route road, a gravel road on the right. There is a power substation by this road. Turn right onto Mail Route road and travel 3.6 miles down Battle Creek Canyon to the junction with a paved road.

Turn left onto this paved road and travel 0.9 miles, then turn right onto the next road and travel 0.5 miles, then turn left onto 1600 West and travel 0.3 miles, then turn right onto 6400 North and travel 1.0 miles to the JUNCTION (6.3 miles) with US 91.

Turn left onto US 91 and travel south a short distance to a creek which crosses under US 91. This is Battle Creek, and the field to the right is the location of the 14 AUGUST CAMPSITE on Battle Creek, four miles from the Bear River. Continue south to the JUNCTION (4.2 miles) with a gravel road on the right.

Turn right onto this gravel road and travel 0.2 miles to a fork in the road. The stream at the fork is Battle Creek. The Bear River Massacre took place in the area from the mouth of the ravine on the north to the Bear River on the south. The massacre occurred on 29 January 1863 between a band of Northwestern Shoshone Indians and soldiers from newly founded Camp Douglas in Salt Lake City, commanded by Colonel Patrick Edward Connor. The massacre was prompted by harassment of overland travelers, settlers, and miners by the Indians, whose traditional lands were rapidly being preempted by the whites. Approximately 250 Indian men, women, and children were killed, along with fourteen soldiers. Many soldiers were afflicted by the extremely cold weather. There is a monument to the Bear River Massacre on the east side of US 91, just north of the Bear River bridge.

Travel down the left-hand fork. Note the deep ravines on the right as you travel the next 4.0 miles. These ravines caused the emigrants to travel in almost every direction. One mile from the fork the road changes from gravel to pavement. Continue on the pavement 0.3 miles to the second fork in the road. Take the left-hand fork, a gravel road, and travel 1.1 miles to the junction with a paved road.

Turn left onto the paved road and travel 1.7 miles to the junction with an east-west road. Turn right onto this road and travel 1.3 miles to the junction with 3200 West. Turn left onto 3200 West and travel south 4.6 miles to the junction with 3600 South. Turn right onto 3600 South and travel 0.4 miles, past a railroad track, to the junction with SR 84. Turn right onto SR 84 and travel 1.0 miles to WESTON (11.5 miles).

The 15 AUGUST CAMPSITE is located just south of Weston on Weston Creek, three miles from the Bear River. Bidwell and John both described the scene. John Bidwell wrote:

> Continued our journey over hills and ravines, going to almost every point of the compass, in order to pass them. having come about 15 miles, we encamped on a small stream proceeding out of the Mountains at no great distance from us. But we were surprised to see it become perfectly dry in the course of an hour, some of the guard said there was plenty of water in it about midnight.

James John wrote: "today we did not travel for perhaps not more than 8 miles on a straight line but the way was rough and winding and hilly we encamped on a small branch about 3 miles from the river that is from Bear river."

Travel south on SR 84 from the east-west road (3600 South) to the UTAH-IDAHO BORDER (2.6 miles). Crossing the border, Idaho SR 84 becomes Utah SR 23. The Bidwell-Bartleson party traveled south along the west side of the Bear River through today's towns of Cornish, Trenton, Amalga, and Newton.

Travel south on SR 23 through Cornish to the JUNCTION (5.7 miles) with SR 142.

Turn left onto SR 142 and travel east 1.5 miles through Trenton to the junction with a road heading south. As you travel towards the junction, SR 142 bends southward and then eastward.

Turn right at the junction and travel south 1.8 miles to the junction with a road on the left. Turn left and travel east 1.5 miles to the junction with a road on the right. Turn right and travel south 1.7 miles to the 16 AUGUST CAMPSITE (6.7 miles), on the left by the Bear River near the town of Amalga. James John described the campsite: "Today we travelled about 10 miles and encamped on the bank of Bear river near a place called Cash valley."

Continue south 1.3 miles to the junction with SR 218. Turn right onto SR 218 and travel 4.0 miles west, then 3.0 miles northwest to NEWTON (8.3 miles). Construction began in 1871 on the first storage reservoir in Utah, now called Newton Reservoir, located just north of the town. South of Newton is Cutler Reservoir, formed by Cutler Dam on the Bear River.

Unable to see where the Bear River crossed the mountains to the west, the Bidwell-Bartleson party traveled along the north bank of the Bear River until they came to the narrows, and then crossed what is now called Long Divide.

Travel through Newton to the junction with SR 142. Turn right onto SR 142 and travel northwest 1.2 miles to the junction with a gravel road on the left. Turn left onto this gravel road, and travel 1.0 miles to the junction with a northeast-southwest gravel road. Turn left onto this curving gravel road, and travel west 5.2 miles over Long Divide to the junction with 2800 West. Turn left onto 2800 West and travel south 1.8 miles until the ROAD BENDS (9.3 miles) westward. The 17 AUGUST CAMPSITE is about one mile to the southwest on the banks of the Bear River.

James John described the river and the falls: "today we travelled about 20 miles and encamped in Cash valley on the bank of Bear river 2 miles blow the falls of that river here the river runs through a deep cut in the Mountain which is narrow and nearly perpendicular and about 300 ft high." Cutler Dam, built just below the falls, impounds the Bear River and its Cache Valley tributaries. The Union Pacific Railroad cuts through these narrows on the south side of the dam.

Travel west through Fielding to the MALAD RIVER (2.5 miles). There is some irrigated land, large areas of dry farms, and grazing land on neighboring hills. When the country was first reconnoitered in 1877, it was covered with sage to the height of a mounted man's head.

The Malad River drains south from Idaho into Utah and joins the Bear River just north of Corinne. Donald Mackenzie, a French Canadian trapper for the Hudson's Bay Company, is given credit for naming the river. He and his men became ill after eating beaver meat. "Malade" is French for "sick." Frémont called the river "Roseaux." Though narrow, this river was a big obstacle for early travelers because of its steep high banks and muddy bottom. The main crossing was Rocky Ford, southwest of the town of Plymouth. This ford had been used for centuries by the Indians, and was used later by the mountain men and overland emigrants.

Continue west to the JUNCTION (0.5 miles) with SR 13.

Optional tour to Rocky Ford (private property). A portion of this optional tour is on private property, and permission is required. Turn right onto SR 13, and travel north 3.0 miles to the junction with 19200 North on the left. A sign reading "Belmont Springs" is at this junction. Turn left onto this road, and travel west down a hill, crossing the Malad River. On the left is a hot springs resort called Belmont Springs or Uddy Springs. Continue west 1.0 miles from SR 13 to the junction with a gravel road (6000 West 19200 North). Turn right onto this gravel road and travel 0.5 miles to an unmarked gravel road on the left, in the Malad River bottoms.

This road is on private property, and permission is required to proceed. Travel west on this gravel road 0.3 miles, under an I-15 overpass structure, to some corrals. Park and walk about two hundred feet north to the Malad River crossing. This natural crossing is called ROCKY FORD, so named because of a layer of small rocks in the bottom of the river.

Return to SR 13 past the hot springs. John Bidwell described these hot springs:

> Traveled but a short distance, when we discovered that a deep salt creek prevented our continuing near the river. In ascending this stream in search of a place to cross it, we found on its margin a hot spring, very deep and clear. The day was very warm and we were unable to reach the river, encamped on this salt creek and suffered much for water, the water being so salt we could not drink it, distance 15 miles.

James John also described these hot springs:

> [T]his four noon we came to a muddy deep creek which we could not cross without going nearly a half days journey up it and consequently we travelled about 5 miles today and came down on the opposite bank and encamped there is a number of hot salt springs on the banks of this creek some of them are nearly as hot as boiling water.

Return to SR 13.

Travel south on SR 13 through Riverside to the 18 AUGUST CAMPSITE (6.6 miles). The emigrants camped by the Malad River on the left. This site is five miles from the 17 August campsite. The Bidwell-Bartleson party traveled down the west bank of the Malad River, through today's Riverside, Garland, and Tremonton.

Continue south on SR 13 through Garland and Tremonton to BEAR RIVER CITY (10.3 miles), and the junction with 6400 North. In Bear River City, you will find the Jim Bridger Monument, honoring the frontiersman who came this way by boat to Great Salt Lake.

Turn right onto 6400 North, and travel west, crossing the Malad River and then a railroad track, to the JUNCTION (2.6 miles) with 6800

West. Turn left onto 6800 West, and travel south to the JUNCTION (4.0 miles) with SR 83. The area to the south and to the east is where the Bidwell-Bartleson party traveled some twelve to thirteen miles in a triangular route looking for Great Salt Lake and fresh water for themselves and their livestock. John Bidwell described this search:

> Started early, hoping soon to find fresh water, when we could refresh ourselves and animals, but alas! The sun beamed heavy on our heads as the day advanced, and we could see nothing before us but extensive arid plains, glimmering with heat and salt, at length the plains became so impregnated with salt, that vegetation entirely ceased; the ground was in many places white as snow with salt & perfectly smooth — the mid-day sun, beaming with uncommon splendor upon these shining plains, made us fancy we could see timber up on the plains, and wherever timber is found there is water always. We marched forward with unremitted pace till we discovered it was an illusion, and lest our teams should give out we returned from S. to E. and hastened to the river which we reached in about 5 miles. A high mountain overlooked us on the East and the river was thickly bordered with willows — grass plenty but so salt, our animals could scarcely eat it; salt glitters upon its blades like frost. Distance 20 miles.

Continue south on 6800 West to the JUNCTION (1.0 miles) with an unmarked east-west road. Turn left onto this road and travel east to CORINNE, 3.5 miles, location of the 19–20 AUGUST CAMPSITE. The party remained here for two days while they explored the surrounding country. They were ten miles from Great Salt Lake.

The first Gentile (the Mormon term for a non-Mormon) town in Utah, Corinne strived to become a commercial center following completion in 1869 of the transcontinental railroad at nearby Promontory; a steamboat center following construction of the *City of Corinne* and the *Kate Connor*, two unsuccessful steamboats that operated on Great Salt Lake in the early 1870s hauling machinery and ore for the mines south of Great Salt Lake; and a political center following establishment of the first political party to oppose the Mormon People's Party. But events kept the town from fulfilling its promise. A diphtheria epidemic in 1872 devastated the population, and completion in 1903 of the Lucin cutoff trestle across the middle of Great Salt Lake finished the economy.

CORINNE, UTAH TO WENDOVER, UTAH

Before traveling westward to Kelton, Lucin, Donner Spring, and Wendover, *be prepared*. After twenty-five miles of paved road, you will be traveling on gravel roads into desolate desert country. Food, water, and

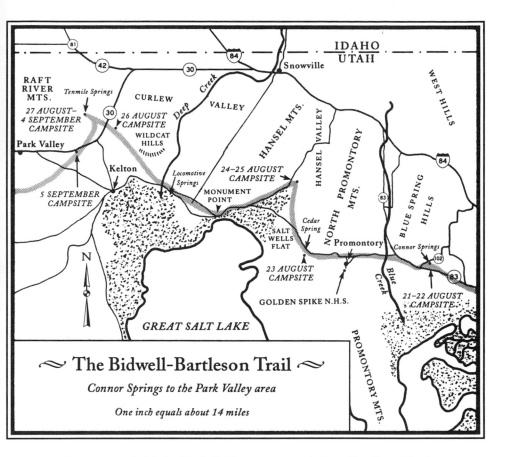

∾ The Bidwell-Bartleson Trail ∾

Connor Springs to the Park Valley area

One inch equals about 14 miles

gasoline are available in Park Valley, seventy-eight miles from Corinne, and in Wendover, eighty-five miles from Park Valley.

The automobile tour starts at the OLD CHURCH in Corinne, located sixty-five miles north of Salt Lake City.

Travel north 0.2 miles to the junction with SR 13. Turn left onto SR 13, then turn left onto SR 83, and travel west to the JUNCTION (14.2 miles) with SR 102.

Optional tour to 21–22 August campsite. Travel 1.7 miles to the northeast until you come to a house on your right. This is Connor Springs, the 21–22 AUGUST CAMPSITE. John Bidwell wrote: "S. 21st. Marched off in a N.W. direction, and intersected our trail of Thursday last, having made a complete triangle in the plain." James John wrote: "21st Travelled about 12 miles and came to a large salt springs where we

camped. 22nd. Stayed in camp on account of our oxen straying. We found them towards evening. The men who went to Fort Hall, 7 in number, returned today. They obtained some provisions but could get no pilot."
Return to SR 83.

Travel west on SR 83 to the JUNCTION (3.5 miles) with a road on the left. This is Lampo Junction, and just north of here is Thiokol's Wasatch Division, an industrial facility devoted to research, development, and manufacture of solid-propellant rocket motors. Occupying more than one hundred brightly colored buildings, the Thiokol plant is the largest of its kind in the world. Interestingly, Thiokol's plant, whose rocket motors are used to launch NASA's space shuttle, is within sight of another transportation landmark — the completion of the nation's first transcontinental railroad.

Turn left at Lampo Junction and travel west 6.7 miles on the paved road. Take the right-hand fork up the hill past railroad cuts and fills to where the pavement turns left. The road to the left goes south 1.2 miles to GOLDEN SPIKE NATIONAL HISTORIC SITE (7.9 miles). Golden Spike National Historic Site marks Promontory Summit, the place where the Union Pacific and Central Pacific railroads met on 10 May 1869, to form the nation's first transcontinental railroad.

The culmination of the nation's dream to unite the east and west coasts brought major changes to the country. The new railroad provided the first practical means of round-trip travel. New opportunities for commerce brought buffalo hunters, who depleted the great bison herds that roamed the plains; it was not long before the bison, and the Plains Indians who hunted them, virtually disappeared. The railroad also advanced the settlement of Nebraska, Wyoming, Colorado, Utah, Nevada, and California, as immigrants in search of fertile farmland rode the rails west by the thousands.

A visitor's center straddles the summit's viewing area where two replica locomotives — Jupiter and Engine 119 — face each other as they did at the 1869 joining of the rails. Each year on 10 May, the joining of the rails ceremony is reenacted for the public. Travel back 1.2 miles to the bend in the pavement.

Travel west on the gravel road past a summit down to CEDAR SPRINGS (4.8 miles), on the left. From here is seen the vista of Great Salt Lake that Bidwell saw from their 23 AUGUST CAMPSITE. John Bidwell described the view: "At evening we arrived in full view of the Salt Lake, water was very scarce. Cedar grows here both on the hills and in the valleys, distance 20 miles." James John also described the view: "Camped at night at a small spring where we did not get half enough water for the animals. We are near the Salt Lake and frequently travelled over plains covered with salt which is good for use."

With the exception of the Dead Sea, Great Salt Lake is the saltiest body of water on Earth. Occupying a large part of northern Utah, the lake is seventy-two miles long and thirty miles wide, but only ten to thirty feet deep. The only crossing over the lake is the 102-mile Southern Pacific Railroad cutoff between Ogden and Lucin.

Centuries ago, the northwestern quarter of Utah was covered by Lake Bonneville, a great freshwater lake ten times the size of Great Salt Lake. Covering more than twenty-thousand square miles in Utah, Nevada, and Idaho, the lake was one thousand feet deep where Great Salt Lake now lies and nine hundred feet deep at the site of Salt Lake City. Lake Bonneville left a distinct shoreline that is still visible. The lake broke through its barrier at the outlet, Red Rock Pass, north of the Battle Creek campsite in Idaho, and with a change in climate the huge lake fell below its lowest outlet and shrank to today's Great Salt Lake. Depending on the water level, Great Salt Lake's salinity varies from 15 to 25 percent, at least six times saltier than the ocean.

A few of the islands in Great Salt Lake are inhabited by wildlife. The largest island, Antelope Island, named by John C. Frémont in 1845, provides a refuge for about five hundred American Bison. Pronghorn antelope and elk have been re-introduced recently to Antelope Island, which is now a state park.

Great Salt Lake rose over twelve feet between 1967 to 1983, covering I-80, Saltair beaches, the roads to Antelope Island, and wildlife refuges. Road grades were raised, dikes built, and pumps installed to pump the high water into the Great Salt Lake Desert. The lake has since receded.

The Great Salt Lake Desert, west of Great Salt Lake, is part of the bed of ancient Lake Bonneville and is composed of clay washed into the huge lake thousands of years ago. At the Bonneville Salt Flats, a low place in this basin located east of Wendover, Utah, salt has been deposited over time. The water from the pumping project covered approximately eight hundred square miles of the Great Salt Lake Desert with salt water, which has since evaporated, leaving a salt crust averaging about six inches thick and covering the Donner-Reed trail.

Follow the unmarked gravel road as it turns northwest to a FORK (9.6 miles) in the road, on the right.

Optional tour to 24–25 August campsite (private property). This optional tour is on private property, and permission is required. This road goes northeast to the 24–25 AUGUST CAMPSITE at Salt Wells. James John described this campsite: "This morning we were detained by the oxen straying. Did not get them till about 12 o'clock. Travelled about 10 miles and camped near a number of salt springs not far from the Lake. These springs are deep. Some of our horses would have drowned had we not seen them in time. There are also extensive plains here which border on the Lake."
Return to the unmarked gravel road.

Continue west on the left-hand fork of the gravel road to MONUMENT POINT (4.7 miles), where Great Salt Lake, the railroad grade, and the Bidwell-Bartleson Trail meet.

Continue northwest to the "Locomotive Springs" SIGN (4.2 miles). South 1.5 miles is the Locomotive Springs State Waterfowl Management Area. The Bidwell-Bartleson party missed these springs, forcing them to travel a long distance and establish a camp without water to the northwest. Locomotive Springs is southeast of Kelton. The springs pour out their waters from the center of a large flat, creating thousands of acres of marsh land, wild hay fields, and sloughs. Thousands of brant, snipe, and ducks frequent the marshes, which are protected as a migratory bird refuge.

Continue west at the Locomotive Springs sign. As you travel west, the road switches to the old Central Pacific Railroad grade. Travel along this grade to the old town site of KELTON (10.3 miles). There are several Bureau of Land Management interpretive signs placed next to the railroad grade that outline the area's railroad history.

Kelton was established as a railroad town. Water was piped in square, hollowed-out timber pipes from a spring to the northwest and used for the steam locomotives. Originally on the Central Pacific Railroad as a stage and freighting station, Kelton served as a major junction for stage and freight lines from Idaho and Oregon. After the Lucin Cutoff was built across Great Salt Lake, the town of Kelton died. The cemetery and old Central Pacific roadbed are all that remain today.

Turn right and travel north from Kelton to the JUNCTION (8.5 miles) with paved SR 30. Turn right onto SR 30 and travel to MILEPOST 66 (1.1 miles), at the junction with an unmarked gravel road on the left. East of this point 2.5 miles is the 26 AUGUST CAMPSITE. John Bidwell described this campsite:

Traveled all day over dry, barren plains, producing nothing but sage, or rather it ought to be called, wormwood, and which I believe will grow without water or soil. Two men were sent ahead in search of water, but returned a little while before dark unsuccessful. Our course intersected an Indian trail, which we followed directly north towards the mountains, knowing that in these dry countries, the Indian trails always lead to the nearest water. Having traveled till about 10 o'clock P.M. made a halt, and waited till morning distance about 30 miles.

Turn left onto the gravel road, and travel north 0.8 miles to a junction, then travel left through a gate 1.4 miles to a locked gate. Northwest of this gate, you can see the meadows at Tenmile Springs. This is the 27 AUGUST – 4 SEPTEMBER CAMPSITE. The Bidwell-Bartleson party stayed at this campsite longer than any other site on the trail. John Bidwell described the reasons for this long rest:

Daylight discovered to us a spot of green grass on the declivity of the mountain towards which we were advancing. 5 miles took us to this place, where we found to our great joy, an excellent spring of water and an abundance of Grass — here we determined to continue, 'till the route was explored to the head of Mary's River and run no more risks of perishing for want of water in this desolate region.

James John also described this campsite:

Started early and travelled about 5 miles, camped. Plenty water and grass here. We remained several days. Some Snake Indians camped near us and came out and traded some berries for powder and buffalo and bullets. The Captain, and an other man named Charles Hopper, left camp on the 30th for the purpose of finding Mary's River. There is neither rain nor, I can here discover, of the season of the year. We have had no rain since we left the Platte River.

Return to SR 30. Turn right onto SR 30, and travel south to a ranch road on the left and the "Morris Ranch" SIGN (4.3 miles).

Location of 5 September campsite (private property). The ranch house is about one-half mile below the hill amongst the cedar trees. This is the 5 SEPTEMBER CAMPSITE. This campsite is located on private property, and the owner (1993) does not want to be disturbed.

Bidwell and John both describe the campsite. John Bidwell wrote: "Grass having become scarce, we concluded to move on a little every day to meet Capt. B. & H. Traveled about 6 miles and encamped by a beautiful Cedar grove." James John wrote: "Left the camp that we came to on the 27th of August and went about 6 miles, camped in a cedar grove

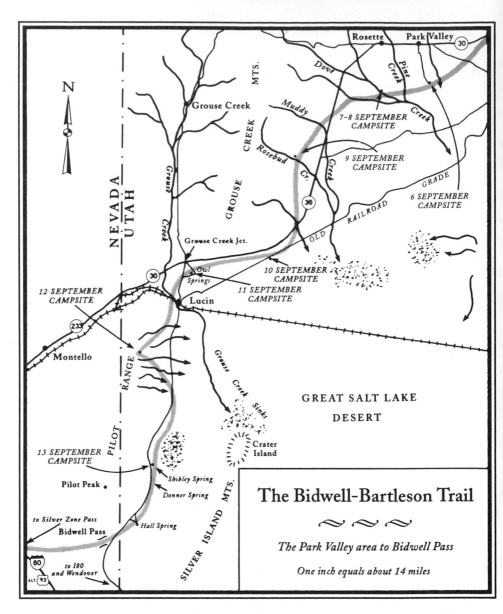

The Bidwell-Bartleson Trail

~ ~ ~

The Park Valley area to Bidwell Pass

One inch equals about 14 miles

near a spring of water and in sight of the plains which border on the Salt Lake. Captain Bartleson and Mr. Hopper have not yet returned."

Travel west on SR 30 through Park Valley to the PALMER TWINS SERVICE STATION (6.6 miles).

Optional tour to 6 September campsite (private property). This optional tour is on private property, and permission is required. There is a gravel

road south of the Palmer Twins Service Station. Travel south and east on this gravel road 5.0 miles. You will come to some trees at Baker Spring, the 6 SEPTEMBER CAMPSITE. John Bidwell described this camp-site: "We travelled about 10 miles a day in a southwest direction and camped on a small brook. Today we killed some rabbits and an antelope. Game being scarce here we were compelled to kill oxen."
Return to SR 30.

Continue west to ROSETTE (4.5 miles). Directly south of Rosette seven miles is the 7–8 SEPTEMBER CAMPSITE.

Continue southwest to MILEPOST 37 (17.8 miles). You will see an emigrant road which crosses the highway from northeast to southwest. The Bidwell-Bartleson party is believed to have pioneered this road.

Continue southwest to ROSEBUD SPRINGS (4.1 miles) to an un-marked gravel road on the right. Turn right onto the gravel road and travel west 1.3 miles, then travel right at a fork 1.0 miles to a locked metal gate. The buildings behind this gate comprise a Bureau of Land Man-agement camp. This is the 9 SEPTEMBER CAMPSITE. John Bidwell wrote: "The part of the Company that remained yesterday, went on and overtook the 2 wagons. Capt. Bartleson & Hopper returned, bringing Intelligence that they had found the head of Mary's river — distant about 5 days travel, distance traveled to day about 12 miles S. W. direction. The Indians stole a horse — day cool." Return to SR 30.

Continue southwest to a HISTORICAL MARKER (3.5 miles), on the left. Travel 7.0 miles until you come to a slight bend in the road. South of this bend one mile is the 10 SEPTEMBER CAMPSITE. James John wrote: "This morning the Indians were dismissed and we gave them some powder and lead balls which appeared to satisfy them for their service. We travelled about 14 miles today and then camped near the foot of a mountain with neither water nor grass for our animals."

Continue southwest to the Grouse Creek JUNCTION (14.0 miles). Turn left and follow the southeast unmarked road 1.2 miles to the trees at Owl Springs. This is the 11 SEPTEMBER CAMPSITE. James John described the campsite: "We started early, travelled about 14 miles to the southwest, and found water and grass here and we camped for the night."

The following day, the first wagons were abandoned. John Bidwell wrote: "Mr. Kelsey left his wagons and took his family and goods on pack horses, his oxen not being able to keep up: distance to day about 12 miles." James John wrote: "This morning left two wagons belonging to B. Kelsey, their oxen being worn down by fatigue. They were compelled to leave their wagons and pack their belongings on horses and mules."

Continue southeast 0.1 miles to the junction with a road that goes southwest. Travel 0.3 miles on this road to where a wagon trail crosses to the southwest. This trail was probably established by the Bidwell-Bartleson party traveling from the spring. Continue southwest 0.9 miles to the JUNCTION (2.5 miles) with the Lucin/Wendover road.

Travel south on the Lucin/Wendover road 3.3 miles to the old Central Pacific Railroad grade and a historical sign. Continue southwest 0.8 miles to where the road crosses the Southern Pacific Railroad tracks. On the south side of the railroad, and east of the road crossing, is LUCIN (4.1 miles). Occupied by employees of the Central Pacific and Southern Pacific railroads, Lucin was a small railroad town on the west side of the Great Salt Lake Desert. Today, the railroad crosses Great Salt Lake. The town's name comes from a local fossil (Lucina subanta).

Continue south to the SUMMIT (5.8 miles) of the hill, where there is a dirt road going to a spring at the foot of the mountain. This spring is the 12 SEPTEMBER CAMPSITE. James John wrote: "We travelled about 10 miles today southwest and camped at a excellent spring near a large plain covered with salt partly surrounded by high mountains."

Continue south on the Lucin/Wendover road. A wagon trail crosses the road at 4.2 miles from the northeast and then crosses again going southeast. This trail probably was established by the Bidwell-Bartleson party. There is an ABANDONED HOUSE (4.7 miles) on the right. Continue southeast then south to SHIBLEY SPRINGS (10.5 miles), on the left. This is the 13 SEPTEMBER CAMPSITE. John Bidwell wrote: "Traveled about 15 miles south, between Salt plains on the E. and high mtns. on the W."

Continue south to the TL BAR RANCH (4.5 miles), where Donner Spring is located by the dead trees. Continue southwest to the JUNCTION (4.7 miles) with the Hall Springs road.

Turn left onto the Hall Springs Road and travel southwest to HALL SPRINGS (0.6 miles). The Bidwell-Bartleson party had dinner here on 14 September. James John wrote: "We started early this morning and passed a number of good springs, took dinner at one of them." Return to the Lucin/Wendover road.

To the west is 10,700-foot Pilot Peak. Named by John C. Frémont, Pilot Peak is in Nevada, close to the Utah-Nevada border. The peak was a landmark to all emigrant parties moving west in this part of the country. Explorers, mountain men, trappers, and Indians also used the peak as their guide. It could be seen from great distances as emigrant parties crossed the Great Salt Lake Desert.

Continue southwest on the Lucin/Wendover road 5.9 miles to where the Bidwell-Bartleson party trail crosses the gravel road from east to west. This is where Edwin Bryant, traveling ten miles southwest of Donner Spring, saw an old wagon road on 5 August 1846. Bryant wrote: "After travelling about ten miles we struck a wagon-trail, which evidently had been made several years." He then recollected an expedition by Bartleson and Chiles, another member of the 1841 party that went to California.

Continue southeast and at 1.5 miles look westward where you will see a low pass, recently named Bidwell Pass. West of Bidwell Pass 7.5 miles is the 14 SEPTEMBER CAMPSITE. John Bidwell wrote: "Traveled about 25 miles and stopped about 9 o'clock at night, in the middle of a dry plain, destitute of water." Four miles west from the 14 September campsite is a small spring in Silver Zone Pass, and about fifteen miles further west is Big Springs, the 15 SEPTEMBER CAMPSITE, at the foot of the Pequop Range. This is where the Bidwell-Bartleson party abandoned the rest of their wagons before continuing on to California.

Continue southeast over Leppy Pass, down the other side of the mountain to the salt flats, to the JUNCTION (12.0 miles) with a curved paved road. The paved road heading east goes 3.0 miles to the Bonneville Salt Flats. The paved road heading south goes to the JUNCTION (1.4 miles) with I-80. At this point you are 117 miles west of Salt Lake City and 3 miles east of the Utah-Nevada border.

The Pioneer Trail

Jack B. Tykal

The Needles, prominent landmark near the head of Echo Canyon.
Photograph by Charles Kelly, from Photograph Archives, Utah State Historical Society.

HISTORICAL PERSPECTIVE

Established by Jim Bridger and Louis Vasquez at its present location in 1843, Fort Bridger was the first emigrant way station west of Fort Laramie, and the only way station between Fort Laramie and Sutter's Fort on the Sacramento River for those emigrants not traveling by way of Fort Hall. It was built primarily to supply westbound emigrants, but it also conducted a trade with the Indians. Most California–bound emigrant trains that stopped at Fort Bridger for supplies took a northerly route via City of Rocks and then dropped south to the Humboldt River. A short cut was espoused in 1844 by Lansford W. Hastings that ran from Fort Bridger to Salt Lake Valley, and across the Great Salt Lake Desert to the Humboldt River, where it joined the California Trail coming down from the City of Rocks near present-day Wells, Nevada.

The fort was purchased from Bridger and Vasquez by the Mormons in 1855, and was burned by them in 1857 to prevent its being used by Johnston's army as a wintering ground. It was taken over as a military post in 1858, and built to the design that the visitor sees today. There is little remaining evidence of the fur trade or emigrant era, although recent archeological efforts have unearthed what appears to be part of Bridger's original trading post.

William Clayton, a member of the first Mormon train, described the fort in 1847:

> Bridger's fort is composed of two double log houses about forty feet long each and joined by a pen for horses about ten feet high constructed by placing poles upright in the ground close together, which is all the appearance of a fort in sight. There are several Indian lodges close by and a full crop of young children playing around the door. These Indians are said to be of the Snake tribe, the Utahs inhabiting beyond the Mountains. ... Fort Bridger [is] above the level of the sea according to Elder [Orson] Pratt's observation 6,665 ft. It is doubtless a very cold region and little calculated for farming purposes.

Edwin Bryant described the fort in 1846 as being "two or three log cabins, rudely constructed, and bearing but faint resemblance to habitable houses."

George Shepard, a California gold rush emigrant, described the fort's setting in 1850:

> [I]t is a small valley with a large creek running through it surrounded on all sides by high bluffs and mountains ... on the south the mountains are white with snow and the high bluffs are barren places but the valley is green with grass and bushes and trees along side the creek and dotted all over with cattle and horses.

Bridger, himself, described his post in an 1843 letter to Pierre Chouteau, Jr. (keeping in mind that Bridger could neither read nor write):

> I have established a small fort with a blacksmith shop and a supply of iron, on the road of the immigrants on Black's Fork of Green River which promises fairly. They, in coming out, are generally well supplied with money, but by the time they get here are in want of all kinds of supplies. Horses, provisions, smith-work, &c, bring ready cash from them, and should I receive the goods hereby ordered will do a considerable business in that way with them. The same establishment trades with the Indians in the neighborhood who have mostly a good number of beaver with them.

Fort Bridger was an important location on the early trail to Oregon and California. Once beyond Fort Bridger, the trails followed the dictates of geography, weather, convenience, and varying burdens of travel. After passing through Echo Canyon, the 1846 emigrants following the Hastings Cutoff traveled by various routes via Weber Canyon, East Canyon, and Emigration Canyon to Salt Lake Valley. (See "The Hastings Cutoff" chapter below for more information on the 1846 emigrants.)

The 1846 Donner-Reed party followed the route to Salt Lake Valley via East Canyon, Big Mountain, Little Mountain, and Emigration Canyon. The Mormons followed the same route in 1847 after a scouting party had determined that the Emigration Canyon route avoided the difficult passage of the Weber Canyon route. Unlike the 1846 emigration, however, the Mormons entered Salt Lake Valley to stay.

Salt Lake Valley was well known to the early mountain men and explorers. Etienne Provost had traveled throughout the valley in 1824–26. Members of the Henry-Ashley fur company had circumnavigated Great Salt Lake in 1825–26. At a meeting with Jim Bridger between Fort Laramie and Fort Bridger, the Mormons had received a firsthand report about Salt Lake Valley. When the Mormons arrived in 1847, Miles Goodyear had a trading post in operation in the area of today's Ogden.

Although it was a difficult route, the Mormon immigrants that followed the July 1847 pioneer company continued to use the Pioneer Trail. In 1848, Mormon pioneer Parley P. Pratt began exploring Salt Lake Valley canyons for an easier alternative to the Emigration Canyon route. Pratt's "The Golden Pass! Or, New Road Through the Mountains" was opened on 4 July 1850, in time to serve the California gold rush traffic. The Golden Pass road left the Pioneer Trail at the mouth of Echo Canyon and traveled south up the Weber River to Rockport (now under the waters of Rockport Reservoir). From Rockport, the road turned westward through Parley's Park and down Parley's Canyon to Salt Lake Valley. The route roughly followed today's I-80 from Echo Canyon to Salt Lake City. Nine miles longer than the Emigration Canyon trail, the Golden Pass route was a toll road which saw use only for one year — 1850. The following year, Pratt left Salt Lake City on a Mormon Church mission to Chile. Without his promotion and continued maintenance, the road was soon abandoned.

By 1850, the Emigration Canyon route was a well-traveled highway to Salt Lake Valley, used by the Mormon immigrants, by the parties using the Hastings Cutoff west across the Great Salt Lake Desert, and by those using the Salt Lake Cutoff north to City of Rocks.

FORT BRIDGER, WYOMING TO SALT LAKE CITY

If you start this tour by driving from Salt Lake City to Fort Bridger, there are several sites on the Pioneer Trail that can be seen better while traveling east on I-80. They are indicated here by the mile markers along I-80. Look for them on the eastward trip, and keep them in mind as you work your way westward along the Pioneer Trail.

Utah mile 187, CASTLE ROCK. Pony Express Station location. The Pioneer Trail comes into Echo Canyon just above Castle Rock.
Utah mile 189, CACHE CAVE. To the right, just beyond the ridge, about one mile.
Wyoming mile 24, MUDDY CROSSING. The Pioneer Trail comes over ridge south of old US 30.
Wyoming mile 28, BIGELOW BENCH. From the parking area.
Wyoming mile 30, BRIDGER BUTTE. On the south.

After visiting Fort Bridger, drive to the Jim Bridger General Store to start your drive along the Pioneer Trail to Salt Lake City. You should allow a full day, even if you plan to do no more than just drive the route. If you plan to stop at the many points of interest, you should consider dividing the trip into two stages: Fort Bridger to the mouth of Echo Canyon, and Echo Canyon to Salt Lake City. There is much to explore, and some spectacular views, particularly if you use a four-wheel drive vehicle.

Four primary emigrant groups followed this route in 1846, and the Mormons followed it in 1847. The 1846 groups included the Bryant-Russell, Harlan-Young, Hoppe-Lienhard, and Donner-Reed parties.

The Bryant-Russell party was made up of nine men, all riding mules, so they had few of the logistic problems that the other emigrant trains encountered. Bryant wrote home from Fort Bridger to advise other trains not to take the Hastings route in the future, but noted that he was going to follow it just because they were mounted, had minimal gear, and could move more swiftly than parties hampered by wagons and oxen.

Although the various emigrants did not always follow the same route, they were all heading for Salt Lake Valley. The trails began at Fort Bridger, but in crossing Bigelow Bench they diverged and crossed Muddy Creek in at least two locations. The Bryant-Russell party followed what is now the line of the Union Pacific Railroad to present Evanston, to the north of the Donner-Reed, Harlan-Young, and later Mormon emigrants. The route we are following in this tour is primarily that of the Harlan-Young, Donner-Reed, and Mormon parties. Major separation points on the trail will be noted.

The automobile tour starts at the monument off old US 30, next to the JIM BRIDGER GENERAL STORE, Fort Bridger. Fort Bridger is located in southwestern Wyoming, 112 miles from Salt Lake City.

At the Post Office, turn south onto CR 219, and pass the Fort Bridger cemetery.

Travel south on CR 219 to the JUNCTION (1.3 miles) with CR 217. Turn right onto CR 217, a gravel road. You are now traveling west. At 0.4 miles cross Black's Fork, a Green River tributary. At 1.5 miles stop at the overlook (at the turn — there is a farm on left of viewpoint). The Pioneer Trail runs southwest through the meadows in the valley to the right.

Continue to the JUNCTION (3.3 miles) with CR 212. Turn right onto CR 212. Immediately after making the turn the road heads towards the south end of Bridger Butte. To the left are two landmarks of the Pioneer Trail: Sugarloaf Butte on the near left, and Haystack Butte to the far left. The Pioneer Trail goes between the south end of Bridger Butte and Sugarloaf Butte.

The Pioneer Trail here runs atop the bench to the north of CR 212. At 2.6 miles the Pioneer Trail intersects CR 212, and the road overlays the old trail for a bit. At 3.8 miles the Pioneer Trail separates from CR 212, and runs towards Sugarloaf Butte.

Continue west to the JUNCTION (4.5 miles) with a four-wheel drive road to the top of Bridger Butte.

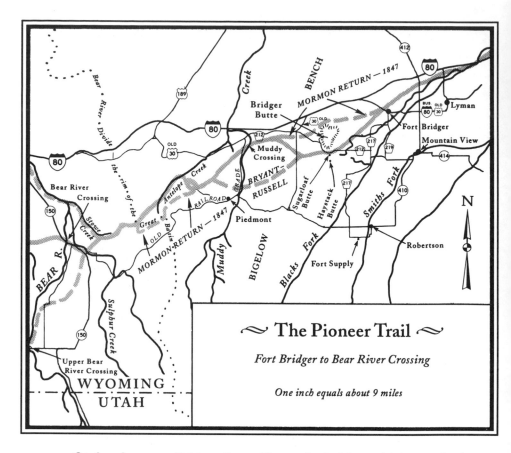

The Pioneer Trail

Fort Bridger to Bear River Crossing

One inch equals about 9 miles

Optional tour to Bridger Butte. Four-wheel drive vehicle required. Turn onto the road and drive to the top of BRIDGER BUTTE. At the top, turn right and follow the gravel road to the overlook point. When the gravel road forks, follow the right fork. The Pioneer Trail can be discerned below, heading to the north of Sugarloaf Butte, and climbing Cottonwood Canyon to Bigelow Bench in a line with the red tower visible in the far distance. Once atop Bigelow Bench, the Pioneer Trail separates, with the main branch crossing the bench approximately one mile north of the Bryant-Russell route.

From the western overlook, drive to the east face of the butte. You can see Fort Bridger from this point, and you can trace the Pioneer Trail around the south end of Bridger Butte. These are magnificent views and an excellent overview of the route the Pioneer Trail followed from Fort Bridger to Bigelow Bench.

Retrace your route to the base of Bridger Butte.

Continue west on CR 212. The Pioneer Trail is now to the left of CR 212. Beginning in 1848, the Pioneer Trail went around the north end of Bridger Butte, and at 1.5 miles this variant crosses CR 212, continuing southwest to join the old trail on Bigelow Bench.

Continue west to the JUNCTION (2.2 miles) with old US 30.

Optional tour to Pioneer Trail remnant. Four-wheel drive vehicle or high-clearance vehicle required. Any vehicle can drive the 2.5 miles to the turnoff, and walk from there. From junction of CR 212 and old US 30, turn south onto Bigelow Bench road. At 2.5 miles, turn left onto the trail through sagebrush. It is difficult to spot, so watch carefully for it. If you come to a wide swath that looks like a wide road crossing in front of you, you've gone too far.

Note the first small rock cairn at 0.3 miles. Follow the right fork 0.1 miles to a second small rock cairn with a ROCK DIRECTION ARROW next to it. This rock arrow is alleged to have been placed there in 1847 by the original Mormon party to point the way over Bigelow Bench to Muddy Creek crossing. Continue 0.1 miles to a third small rock cairn, indicating a fork in the trail coming from Bridger Butte. The right branch heads straight for Medicine Butte.

Retrace your route to the junction of CR 212 and old US 30.

Continue west on CR 212 to the JUNCTION (4.0 miles) with a road to Piedmont and Beartown. Turn left at the crossroads onto the Piedmont road. From here to Beartown, the road is atop the old Union Pacific Railroad bed. The present railroad runs to the right, or north, of the original roadbed, up Antelope Creek to the eastern limit of the Great Basin, and down Stowe Creek to the Bear River, essentially following the route of the Bryant-Russell party.

While driving from the crossroads to the Muddy Creek crossing, look to the left and see where the trails come down off Bigelow Bench. There is a four-wheel drive trail that can be driven to a point below the bench where the trails coming down may be discerned and followed visually to the Muddy Creek crossing.

Travel south on the Piedmont road to the MUDDY CREEK CROSSING (1.6 miles) (sharp right on gravel road to crossing). A Pony Express marker on the west side of Muddy Creek identifies the site of the Moses Byrne Pony Express Station, and a marker reads "Moses Byrne: 1860–1869." A new post contains identifiers on all four sides: Oregon Trail (it was not), California Trail, Mormon Trail, and Pony

Express route. The Bryant-Russell party possibly crossed roughly 1.5 miles south of this crossing.

Return to the Piedmont road. At 3.7 miles are beehive charcoal ovens built by Moses Byrne in 1869 to supply smelters in Salt Lake Valley.

Continue south then west on the Piedmont road to the JUNCTION (4.3 miles) with CR 173. Keep to the right, and you will see a reservoir on the left. Continue to the JUNCTION (5.5 miles) with a four-wheel drive road to a trail remnant.

Optional tour to Pioneer Trail remnant. Four-wheel drive vehicle required. This trail takes you up to the actual trail as it traverses the ridge. Down the other side is a rock bearing the name "Philo Dibble, Jr. Nov 24, 1857." This ridge may be followed west by four-wheel drive vehicles to Beartown, where it joins SR 150. The four-wheel drive path to the ridge follows right on a segment of the Pioneer Trail.

Four-wheel drive vehicles not traveling the ridge should return to the Piedmont road.

Continue west on the Piedmont road to the JUNCTION (14.5 miles) with SR 150. Turn right onto SR 150. At this point, you are approximately forty-one road miles and thirty-one trail miles from Fort Bridger.

Travel north on SR 150. At 1.2 miles is a historical marker describing the railroad history of Bear River City. This is the Sulphur Creek crossing of the Pioneer Trail, and you are back on the actual trail at this point. Brigham Young's camp of 10–11 July 1847 is at this site. The Bryant-Russell party never came to Sulphur Creek, but continued to follow the railroad line toward Evanston. The Bryant-Russell party then followed a route to the north of Echo Canyon, coming back to the Pioneer Trail at Henefer.

From the Sulphur Creek crossing, the Donner-Reed and Harlan-Young parties headed south seven miles on the line of SR 150, then west some two miles to cross the Bear River at the upper crossing (Section 3, T12N, R120W) and pick up Yellow Creek. They followed Yellow Creek towards The Needles at the mouth of Coyote Creek, but turned west short of that spot to head directly towards Emigration Spring, Cache Cave, and thence to Echo Canyon.

James Frazier Reed wrote of their arrival at Sulphur Creek: "on a little creek about 4 miles from Bear River we ought to have turned to the righ[t] and reached Bear Riv[er] in one mile much better road said to be."

Continue north 2.4 miles to a Mormon pioneer marker indicating that Brigham Young and the Mormon party passed this point on 12 July 1847. At 5.0 miles is the Myers Ranch, the oldest ranch in Wyoming.

Continue north to the BEAR RIVER CROSSING (8.6 miles).

Optional tour to Pioneer Trail remnant (private property). This optional tour is on private property, and permission is required. Four-wheel drive vehicle required. To follow the Pioneer Trail, travel 6.3 miles over Myers Ranch land. The trail follows up Stagecoach Hollow to Coyote Creek. The Needles Creek (Coyote Creek) Lienhard camp of 28–29 July 1846 is located 6.5 miles west of the Bear River. The trail exits at The Needles, where it joins Yellow Creek. This is the route followed by the Hoppe-Lienhard party in 1846, and by the Mormons in 1847.
Return to SR 150.

Continue north to the JUNCTION (4.9 miles) with I-80, at Evanston, Wyoming. From Evanston, the Bryant-Russell party rode north down the Bear River for two miles, then west up Thomas Canyon to pick up and follow Crane Creek to the divide between the Bear and Weber rivers. Its members then rode down Trail Creek and Lost Creek to reach the Weber River, near Croydon. Finding Weber Canyon to be impenetrable, they followed the Weber River to Henefer, and took what became the main Pioneer Trail route there.

Travel west on I-80 to Exit 3. Turn left onto US 189.

Travel south on US 189 to the BARKER RANCH (9.4 miles). Look east for a marvelous view of The Needles and the pass coming out of the hills to the flats. The Needles Rock Pony Express station was near Yellow Creek, north of the Barker Ranch.

Continue south to the PIONEER TRAIL CROSSING (1.0 miles). In 1993, the fence line followed the old trail from The Needles to the highway.

Optional tour to The Needles-Echo Canyon overlook (Private Property). This optional tour is on private property, and permission is required. At this point, on the right is a road climbing to the west, up a hill. If you drive through the gate to the top of the rise, you will have a magnificent view of the Pioneer Trail where it exits at The Needles, and you can follow it along the line from that point to where it joins I-80 down Echo

Canyon. Looking south of The Needles, you can approximate the route of the Donner-Reed party coming down Yellow Creek and cutting northwest to the head of Echo Canyon.

Return to US 189.

Travel north back towards Evanston to the JUNCTION (1.4 miles) with CR 151, also identified as Wasatch road. Turn left (northwest) onto CR 151 to the head of Echo Canyon and the JUNCTION (4.2 miles) with I-80. Turn west (downhill).

Travel west on I-80 to CACHE CAVE (4.0 miles). Cache Cave was given its name for the practice of the early trappers to cache their extra supplies there. The 1847 Mormon train passed by, and Orson Pratt described the cave:

> Here is the mouth of a curious cave in the centre of a coarse sandstone fronting to the south. . . . The opening resembles very much the doors attached to an out-door cellar, being about 8 feet high and 12 or 14 feet wide. We called it Reddin's Cave, a man by that name [Return Jackson Redden] being one of the first in our company who visited it. We went into this cave about 30 feet, where the entrance becoming quite small, we did not feel disposed to penetrate it any further.

The cave was given its present name apparently by William Clayton in 1848. The cave is on private land, and the present owner (1993) does not grant permission to cross his land and visit the cave.

Continue west on I-80. At 5.4 miles the Pioneer Trail intersects I-80. The Pioneer Trail now continues down Echo Canyon to Echo Junction.

William Clayton described the canyon in 1847, then called Red Fork Canyon:

> We are yet enclosed by high mountains on each side, and this is the first good camping place we have seen since noon, not for lack of grass or water, but on account of the narrow gap between the mountains. Grass is pretty plentiful most of the distance and seems to grow higher the farther we go west.

> There is a very singular echo in this ravine, the rattling of wagons resembles carpenters hammering at boards inside the highest rocks. The report of a rifle resembles a sharp crack of thunder and echoes from rock to rock for some time. The lowing of cattle and braying of mules seem to be answered beyond the mountains. Music, especially brass instruments, have a very pleasing effect and resemble a person standing inside the rock imitating every note. The echo, the high rocks to the north, high mountains on the south with the narrow ravine for a road, form a scenery at once romantic and more interesting than I have ever witnessed.

William H. Knight was camped in the canyon in 1859 with his emigrant party and he, "fired a shot from my pistol, and we were able to count 21 echoes, each one a little fainter than the preceding, till the last was almost inaudible."

George Shepard described his view of Echo Canyon in 1850:

Head of Echo Crick on the right hand side of the road. . . . followed the crick down a deep ravine 21 1/2 miles with high ridges on each side high and almost perpindicular rock on the right and high gravelly hills on the left my eyes ache and my head swims looking up at these lofty mountains. . . . crossed the creek good many times and very bad crossings

The story is told that the canyon was named "Echo" by Jim Bridger, who, when en route from Salt Lake Valley to Fort Bridger on Black's Fork, would make his first night's camp at the mouth of the canyon. When ready for bed, he would shout up the canyon, "time to get up, Jim," and retire. The echo would bounce back down the canyon at dawn to wake him up.

Others commented, as William Clayton did, on the presence of grass as the pioneers moved westward. Edwin Bryant wrote, "The country through which we have passed today has . . . presented a more fertilized aspect than any we have seen for several hundred miles. Many of the hill-sides and . . . table-land on the high plains produce grass and other green vegetables."

Continue west on I-80 to CASTLE ROCK (7.9 miles). Nearby is the Canyon Pony Express station. Immediately north of the present Castle Rock I-80 exit is the site of Brigham Young's 15 July 1847 camp. Approximately 1.6 miles west of the Castle Rock (Mormon) camp is the site of the Hastings-Clyman, Hoppe-Lienhard, and Donner-Reed camps of 1846.

Continue west on I-80. From 5.0 miles to 6.0 miles, 1857 Mormon War fortifications can be seen on the bluffs to north (right side) of I-80. Look carefully, they are hard to spot.

Continue west to EXIT 169 (9.5 miles) ("Echo"). Travel through Echo and follow the Weber River valley towards Henefer. Some believe the Weber (pronounced "Weeber") River was named for Captain John G. Weber, an early member of William H. Ashley's fur brigades; however, there is some thought that the river may have been named for Pauline Weaver, an early New Mexico and Arizona frontiersman.

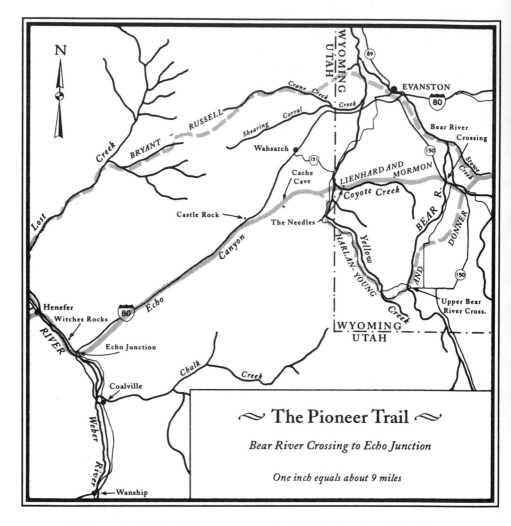

N

RUSSELL

BRYANT

Creek

Lost

Castle Rock →

Canyon

Echo

Henefer
Witches Rocks

Echo Junction

Coalville

RIVER

Weber River

← Wanship

Crane Creek

Creek

Shearing *Corral*

Wahsatch

Cache
Cave

The Needles

Chalk *Creek*

Coyote Creek

LIENHARD AND MORMON

HARLAN-YOUNG

Yellow

Creek

**WYOMING
UTAH**

EVANSTON

Bear River
Crossing

BEAR R.

DONNER

Stout Creek

Upper Bear
River Cross.

~ **The Pioneer Trail** ~

Bear River Crossing to Echo Junction

One inch equals about 9 miles

Where the Weber River passes under I-80 is the site of the Donner-
Reed camp of 6–10 August 1846. At 2.3 miles on the right are the Witches
Rocks. At 4.6 miles is the Weber Canyon explorers trail marker.

From this point in 1846, the Harlan-Young party joined with the
Hoppe-Lienhard party and continued down the Weber River, guided by
Lansford Hastings and fighting their way through the underbrush at the
narrows. They followed the Weber River to the area of today's Ogden,
and then turned south to Salt Lake Valley and around the south end of
Great Salt Lake. The Bryant-Russell party traveled up Main Canyon to
today's East Canyon Reservoir before turning back to the Weber River
at Morgan.

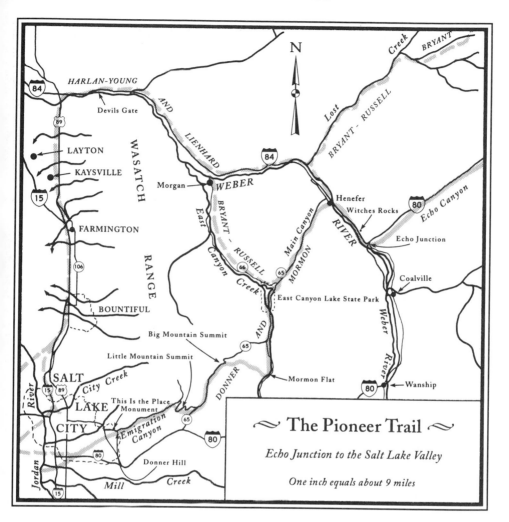

~ The Pioneer Trail ~

Echo Junction to the Salt Lake Valley

One inch equals about 9 miles

Continue to the JUNCTION (5.1 miles) of old US 30 and a blacktop road entering from the left. Leave the main road, and turn left onto the blacktop road that enters old US 30 where it bends right into the town of Henefer.

Continue on the paved road to the GRAVEL ROAD (0.3 miles). Turn left onto the gravel road. The paved road makes a right turn at this point.

Continue on the gravel road to the WEBER RIVER CROSSING OVERLOOK (0.25 miles). At this point a wide turn is on the right side (at the edge of a hayfield in 1993), which gives an excellent overview of the Weber River. The crossing site is 45° to the left as you face the river.

George Shepard encountered this crossing in 1850: " . . . came to Weber river ford . . . the water is high and there are some Mormons here to ferry emigrants over . . . they have a raft instead of a boat and take 3 dollars to carry over a wagon and then we have to swim the horses."

Shepard's party apparently objected to the $3 toll, so they explored a ford some fifty rods downstream; however, after witnessing the difficulties encountered by a party crossing the ford, they willingly paid the toll at the ferry.

Retrace your route back to the stop sign at the main road, and turn left into Henefer.

Travel northwest to MAIN CANYON (0.5 miles). Turn left onto SR 65, and travel west up Main Canyon. At 1.7 miles is the Summit historical marker, which was moved from its original location at the junction of the Lincoln Highway (US 30) and the Pioneer Trail at Echo Junction to this location. At 3.3 miles the Lonetree Campsite monument (without a plaque) identifies a Mormon militia campsite from 1857–58. At 4.7 miles, 4.9 miles, and 5.3 miles, traces of the trail may be seen to the right (bare spaces on gully side).

Continue to THE HOGSBACK (5.8 miles). As the pioneers topped the rise from Weber Valley (Henefer), they got their first awesome view of the Wasatch Mountains ahead, which they knew they had to cross. Stop and look to the southwest to see what they saw.

At 1.7 miles is the Dixie Hollow historical marker. At this point, the trail down Dixie Hollow became impassable, so the pioneers turned right, up Broad Hollow, to Broad Bench, which they followed to today's East Canyon Reservoir. The Donner-Reed party camped nearby, as did Orson Pratt's advance party of Mormons in 1847.

Continue to the JUNCTION (2.3 miles) with SR 66.

Optional tour to East Canyon State Park. Travel SR 66 to EAST CANYON STATE PARK. At 0.9 miles to the left (northwest, across the reservoir) is the dam, which is at the narrows that stopped the Bryant-Russell party in 1846. They crossed over the ridge to the right of the dam by way of an Indian trail. The Bryant-Russell party went this way to today's Morgan and to the Weber River route to Salt Lake Valley because they had not enough men to cut their way through the Weber River narrows below today's Henefer.

At 1.2 miles the Pioneer Trail came down the gulch on the right. In 1992 there was a Mormon Trail marker there, and a closed gate with a farm road running up the hill to Broad Bench.

At 1.6 miles is East Canyon State Park. Turn into the park, and use the boat ramp area at the water's edge to turn around. Looking south from here you will have an excellent view up East Canyon and the route of the Donner-Reed party in 1846. The Donner-Reed trail traveled right down the middle of the reservoir.

George Shepard came this way in 1850, and described the trail from Hogsback Ridge: "went down a steep hill and in four miles make Kenyon crick . . . very high banks to descend into and bad crossing."
Return to the junction of SR 66 and SR 65.

Continue to travel southwest on SR 65. At 1.0 miles there is another excellent view of the narrows that blocked the Bryant-Russell party (where the dam is now located) and of the ridge over which they crossed. Look beyond the dam for some idea of how the canyon narrowed in 1846.

Continue south on SR 65 to the JUNCTION (5.6 miles) with the Pioneer Trail. Turn left onto the gravel road. Here the Pioneer Trail follows East Canyon Creek through a series of lovely mountain meadows. Just after starting down this gravel road there are several buildings on the left. This is the alleged site of the Bauchmann Pony Express station; however, this identification probably is in error. The East Canyon station, sometimes called the Bauchmann station, or Snyderville station, is said to be under the waters of East Canyon Reservoir. There is an old log building at this site that may be part of the old station, moved there before the rising water claimed all under it.

Continue south on the gravel road to MORMON FLAT (3.3 miles). Here the Donner-Reed party and the later Mormon pioneers began their climb up Big Mountain after resting and recruiting their livestock at nearby Large Springs. The Pioneer Trail went up the draw beyond the creek, climbing steadily, but not too steeply, to the summit of Big Mountain. From the parking lot, you can look up at the route of the trail and see the breastworks erected on the ridge of nearby bluffs during the 1857 Mormon War by the Mormon defenders against Colonel Albert Sidney Johnston's army.

Optional walking tour to Big Mountain Summit. Cross the bridge over the creek and bear off on the walking trail to the right. After crossing the creek again, on rocks, you will come to a sty over the fence. Beyond are markers identifying the hiking trail that follows atop the Pioneer Trail about 4.0 miles to the Big Mountain summit, a worthwhile hike and, while uphill, not too strenuous.

George Shepard wrote about his ascent of Big Mountain in 1850: "we now ascended a mountain four miles on a steady pull sometimes on the side hill sometimes in the crick and going 3 or 4 rods on nothing but stones before we got at the top of the mountain."

Return to the SR 65 junction.

Continue south on SR 65 to BIG MOUNTAIN SUMMIT (5.6 miles). To the left of the historical marker the hiking trail may be seen emerging from the draw. This is the same route followed by the Pioneer Trail. Go to the other side of the parking area and to a point near the main road. Looking west, towards Salt Lake Valley, is the same view the pioneers had as they caught their first sight of the valley. From that point you can look down a draw, and on down the canyon towards Mountain Dell. This steep descent is the route followed by the wagon trains down Big Mountain.

Again quoting George Shepard in 1850: "went on down the longest and steepest and crookedest hill I ever see."

Continue south on SR 65. At 3.1 miles is a defaced historical marker, which at one time identified the Birch Springs Camp, the campsite of Orson Pratt's advance party of Mormons in 1847. At 5.7 miles is another defaced marker, and this marker probably identified the Ephraim Hanks Pony Express station site. To the left, just at the north end of the reservoir, a clump of trees may mark the Wheaton Springs Pony Express station site. This can be seen clearly from the summit of Little Mountain. Both of these Pony Express station sites are open to question.

Continue south to the JUNCTION (6.0 miles) with the Emigration Canyon road. Turn right onto the Emigration Canyon road to go up Little Mountain.

Continue west on the Emigration Canyon road to LITTLE MOUNTAIN SUMMIT (1.7 miles). The historical marker indicates the Donner-Reed party crossed on 21 August 1846, and the Mormons in July 1847. The Pioneer Trail here follows a route to the right of the present road. From the summit, look back and down towards the dam. The route of the trail may be discerned by following the draw from a point south of the dam (Camp Grant) to the summit.

Continue west on the Emigration Canyon road. At 0.9 miles the trail comes downhill to the right and crosses the present road. It intersects again with the present-day road at DONNER HILL (7.3 miles). The historical marker identifies the point where the Donner-Reed party could no longer fight its way through heavy underbrush and had to turn

left and go up over the ridge to the left of the road (where the condo-
miniums are now located) and down into the valley. The marker indicates that a year later the Mormons cut their way through this stretch in
four hours. The relative ease with which the Mormons made this passage
is in vivid contrast to the trouble the Donner-Reed party faced one year
earlier.

William Clayton described this, the only independent contribution
of the Mormons to what became known as the Mormon Trail:

> [S]o very steep as to be almost impossible for heavy wagons to ascend,
> and so narrow that the least accident might precipitate a wagon down a
> band three or four hundred feet. . . . Two men were sent around the
> blockage to determine what might be done and they said a good road can
> soon be made down the canyon by digging a little and cutting through
> the bushes some ten or fifteen rods. A number of men went to work
> immediately . . . . After spending about four hours labor the brethren
> succeeded in cutting a pretty good road along the creek, and the wagons
> proceeded on . . .

While the rest of the party were clearing the trail, on 22 July, William
Clayton climbed to the top of Donner Hill and looked upon Salt Lake
Valley:

> It is evident that the emigrants who passed this way last year must have
> spent a great deal of time cutting a road through the thickly set timber
> and heavy brush wood.

> While the brethren were cutting the road I followed the old one to the
> top of the hill [Donner Hill] and on arriving there was much cheered by
> a handsome view of the great Salt lake laying as I should judge, from 25
> to 30 miles to the west of us, and at 11 o'clock I sat down to contemplate
> the surrounding scenery. There is an extensive, beautiful level looking
> valley from here to the Lake which I should judge from the numerous
> deep green patches to be fertile and rich. The valley extends to the south
> probably 50 miles where it is again surrounded by high mountains. To the
> South West across the valley at about 20 to 25 miles distance is a high
> mountain extending from the South end of the valley to about opposite
> this place where it ceases abruptly leaving a pleasant view of the dark
> waters of the Lake [Oquirrh Mountains] . . . The intervening valley
> appears to be well supplied with streams, creeks and lakes some of the
> latter are evidently salt. There is but little timber in sight anywhere, and
> that is mostly on the banks of creeks and streams of water which is the
> only objection that could be raised in my estimation to this being one of
> the most beautiful vallies and pleasant places for a home for the Saints
> which could be found.

Continue to THIS IS THE PLACE MONUMENT (1.3 miles) and
Pioneer Trail State Park. Near this point, Brigham Young designated

Salt Lake Valley as the gathering place of the Mormon people. The monument is on the opposite side of Emigration Creek from the actual Pioneer Trail. From the mouth of Emigration Canyon, the Donner-Reed party and the Mormon pioneers went southwest towards today's Sugarhouse area before turning north to what would become Salt Lake City.

Visit the monument and the pioneer village. The village was created from pioneer buildings found elsewhere in Utah and moved to the site. It gives the visitor a sense of what early Salt Lake City must have been like.

The Hastings Cutoff

Rush Spedden

~

Cobb Peak, at the north end of Silver Island, with pioneer tracks across the Bonneville Salt Flats. *Photograph (1964) by Jack Shapiro.*

HISTORICAL PERSPECTIVE

Lansford W. Hastings, a young lawyer from Ohio, traveled over the Oregon Trail with the emigration of 1842 and in the following year went south from Oregon to California where he became enamored with that country. He returned to the states by way of Mexico in 1844 to write his *Emigrants' Guide to Oregon and California*, published in Cincinnati in the spring of 1845, and to lecture on the glories of California. His *Emigrant's Guide* included the following directions:

> Those who go to California, travel from Fort Hall, west southwest about fifteen days, to the northern pass, in the California mountains; thence . . . to the Sacramento. . . . The most direct route, for the California emigrants, would be to leave the Oregon route, about two hundred miles east of Fort Hall; thence bearing west southwest, to the Salt Lake; and thence continuing down to the bay of San Francisco.

The direct route Hastings proposed is today the general corridor for I-80, although the trail that he pioneered was in no way as direct or as easy as he envisioned.

When Hastings learned that many emigrants bound for Oregon were assembling in Independence, Missouri, in the summer of 1845, he went there in the hope of diverting a large number to California under his guidance. He succeeded in gathering a party of only a dozen men that left Independence on 15 August 1845. They packed their equipment so that they could travel rapidly with horses. Their route was by the already established California Trail to Fort Hall and then across to the Humboldt River. They arrived at Sutter's Fort on 25 December 1845.

During the time that Hastings was crossing just to the north of Utah, Captain John C. Frémont with his topographic surveying party was exploring the area around the south shore of Great Salt Lake. In late October 1845 when a storm coated the high mountains around the lake with snow, Frémont decided to head west in order to reach California before being blocked by Sierra snows. He camped at the springs at present Grantsville and at Redlum Spring in Skull Valley. After crossing the Cedar Mountains near Redlum Spring, he followed a nearly straight course across the Great Salt Lake Desert to the northern tip of Silver Island and then northwesterly to Pilot Peak, thus making the first recorded crossing of this section of the Great Salt Lake Desert. Frémont sent most of his party on west and down the Humboldt while he swung south to explore central Nevada. Frémont, himself, reached Sutter's Fort on 10 December 1845.

Lansford Hastings was delighted to learn that Frémont's main group under Lieutenant Theodore Talbot had been able to take a nearly direct route from Great Salt Lake to the Humboldt River and had reported that the route was feasible for wagons. This confirmed his postulation of a "direct route" in his guide. Thus in late April 1846, Hastings together with James Clyman and James M. Hudspeth among others set out to backtrack on the Frémont party trail to the south shore of Great Salt Lake and then to explore a feasible way to reach Fort Bridger. At the end of May, they followed Frémont's tracks across the Great Salt Lake Desert to Skull Valley. James Clyman had explored and trapped in this area as early as 1826 and thus had a general idea of how to reach Fort Bridger. They crossed over the Wasatch Mountains by way of Parleys Canyon, Mountain Dell Canyon, Big Mountain, and East Canyon, thus finding the way by which Hastings was later to direct the Donner-Reed party. They continued up Echo Canyon, passed present Evanston and found their way northeast to the branch of the Oregon Trail going northwest from Fort Bridger.

During the next month, Hastings and Hudspeth were actively engaged in their efforts to divert emigrants at Fort Bridger from the Fort Hall route to his new "Cut-off" to California. With Hudspeth guiding, the first group, the Bryant-Russell mounted party, left Fort Bridger on 17 July 1846. The same day Hastings led the large Harlan-Young wagon train out, and over the next few days several smaller parties followed, a total of perhaps seventy-five wagons. Finally, on 31 July, the Donner-Reed train of twenty-three wagons left the fort area. All the parties, with the exception of the Donner-Reed, reached Salt Lake Valley by going down the Weber River. Due to the great size of James F. Reed's "Prairie Palace" wagon, Hastings advised the Donner-Reed party to take the East Canyon trail by which he himself had come east. One of the smaller parties traveling in the wake of the Harlan-Young train included two men who have left significant details of the Hastings Cutoff. Heinrich Lienhard was a young Swiss who kept a detailed diary that he edited for publication in his later years. Traveling with another wagon, which at many times was with the Lienhard wagon, was a T. H. Jefferson. This man of mystery, about whom little is known, appears to have returned to New York by ship where he published his own guide as the *Map of the Emigrant Road from Independence, Mo., to San Francisco, California* in 1849. The map is amazingly accurate both as to direction and distance.

The bearings of the trail as drawn are those which would be read directly from a compass rather than true bearings as would be used by a surveyor.

All of these emigrants of 1846 worked their way across Salt Lake Valley to the north end of the Oquirrh Mountains and then, by at least two trails, reached the series of springs known as "Twenty Wells" where Grantsville was established a few years later. The main body of the emigration went from here to Pilot Peak in early August. The Donner-Reed party, however, trailed behind due to their difficulties in cutting a wagon road up East Canyon and down Emigration Canyon to Salt Lake Valley. As a result, they didn't attempt the Great Salt Lake Desert crossing until the last of August. Their additional problems encountered on the salt flats, where they lost many oxen and were forced to abandon some wagons, were a major contributing factor to their ultimate disaster in the Sierra Nevada.

Although some of the historical reviews of recent decades have claimed that the publicized troubles of the Donner Party resulted in the early abandonment of the Hastings Cutoff, both Dale L. Morgan and J. Roderic Korns found diaries proving that in July and August of 1850 gold-seekers used this cutoff at the rate of several hundred a day as they were led across the Great Salt Lake Desert to Pilot Peak by guides from Salt Lake City. After Hensley opened the Salt Lake Cutoff to the north of Great Salt Lake, however, many of the California emigrants chose that path after visiting Salt Lake City for resupply. Nevertheless, maps of the 1870s clearly show "Hastings Road," indicating that it continued to serve as access to the west for miners and ranchers.

SALT LAKE CITY TO WENDOVER, UTAH

Visible sections of the Hastings Road may be found only from Exit 77 of I-80 westward to Donner Spring at the base of Pilot Peak. All traces of the pioneer trails in both the Salt Lake and Tooele valleys have been obliterated by farming and urbanization. Although Lansford Hastings came down Weber Canyon with the vanguard of the 1846 emigration, the Donner-Reed trail down Emigration Canyon, followed by the Mormons in 1847, has been known as the route of the Hastings Cutoff because all later travelers came that way.

From the mouth of Emigration Canyon the Donner party took a course southwest to the crossing of the Jordan River in the vicinity of 2700 South Street. From there they went nearly west a short distance south of 2100 South Street to where they joined the tracks of the Harlan-Young party in the vicinity of the Magna junction on 2100 South Street. Hastings and the Harlan-Young party had apparently crossed the Jordan River about where North Temple Street now crosses it and had followed a southwest course across the valley. Thus, in going west from Salt Lake City, you may take either I-80 or 2100 South, and let your imagination visualize the terrain over which the pioneers traveled in reaching the south shore of Great Salt Lake, near Black Rock at Lake Point Junction (I-80 Exit 102, a distance of approximately 21 miles from Temple Square).

The term "Hastings Cutoff" (or Cut-off) was used historically for the general route from Fort Bridger via the south shore of Great Salt Lake to the Humboldt River. The section from Fort Bridger to Salt Lake City became known as the Pioneer Trail, and the section west of Salt Lake City as the Hastings Road. In the last few decades, the Hastings Road has been referred to more commonly as the Donner-Reed Trail, or simply as the Donner Trail.

As was true for the pioneers, you may find a compass useful in locating some of the landmarks and trail segments. Trail markers placed by the Oregon-California Trails Association in 1993–1994 identify many sites along the Hastings Cutoff.

The automobile tour starts at TEMPLE SQUARE in downtown Salt Lake City. Travel west via either I-80 or 2100 South Street to the JUNCTION (21.5 miles) of SR 201 (2100 South Street) and I-80 (Exit 102, "Garfield"). In Great Salt Lake stands Black Rock, a landmark mentioned in some of the pioneer journals. Approximately 0.5 miles west of this interchange on I-80, there are parking lanes on both sides of freeway. Near this point in 1933, two graves were unearthed by highway crews. The remains have since disappeared, making it now impossible to prove whether or not these were the graves of Luke Halloran and John Hargraves, both of whom were in the 1846 group and died near here.

Travel west on I-80 to EXIT 99 (2.0 miles) ("Tooele/Grantsville"). Travel south on SR 138, which is believed to follow closely one of the trails established in 1846. From this point, according to the T. H. Jefferson map, the pioneers took three routes to the "Hasting Wells" campsite (today's Grantsville). Lienhard mentions a freshwater stream, which would be the one that forms the pond to the east of Exit 99. The near

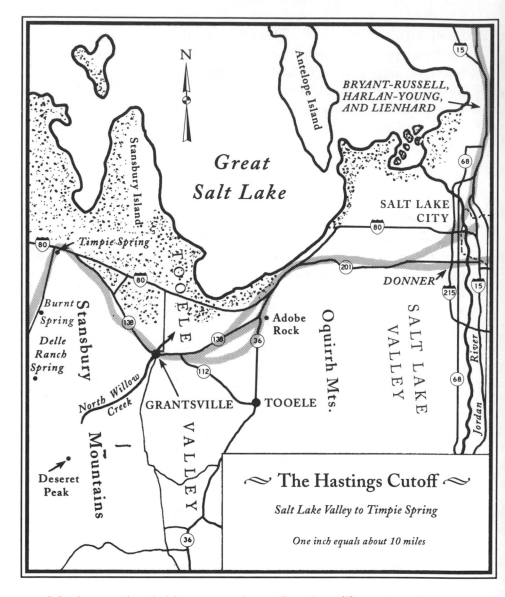

~ The Hastings Cutoff ~

Salt Lake Valley to Timpie Spring

One inch equals about 10 miles

lakeshore trail probably went southwest from here. The main trail, however, went on south along the present highway.

Continue south on SR 138. At 3.3 miles you will see Adobe Rock to the east, another prominent landmark noted in the journals. The junction of SR 138 to Grantsville and SR 38 to Tooele is probably the approximate location of a second fork in the road, as shown on the T. H. Jefferson map. The right-hand branch has apparently become SR 138, which you should follow into Grantsville. The Donner-Reed party, however, continued southward for approximately 2.5 miles before turning west to rejoin the earlier trail. This alternate route became the main road for later emigrants according to the Stansbury map of 1850. The valley floor from Adobe Rock to Grantsville contains several fresh water springs, at one of which the Donner-Reed party camped.

Continue west on SR 138 to the western part of Grantsville, one block past the library, to the DONNER-REED MEMORIAL MUSEUM (14.7 miles), at 97 North Cooley Street. The museum is open by appointment only. Contact Ruth Matthews (801-884-3348) for information. Originally an adobe schoolhouse built in 1861, the museum now displays artifacts recovered from the trail across the Great Salt Lake Desert. Some very large wagon-wheel hubs contribute to the conception that the Reeds' "prairie palace" may have been abandoned on the salt flats.

Clark Street, one block north of Grantsville's main street, is reputed to be the pioneer road along the top of an ancient lake bench. Along the toe of this bench, one to two hundred yards to the north and west, a number of additional springs emerge. Their locations are marked in part by patches of brush or trees, which may be seen from the road west of town. These are "Hasting Wells" of the T. H. Jefferson map or "Twenty Wells" of various pioneer journals.

North Willow Creek runs down to the southwest edge of Grantsville from its canyon on the north flank of Deseret Peak, the highest peak southwest of the town. The Bryant-Russell party riding horses and mules, after camping here and led by Hudspeth, rode up that canyon to the pass over the Stansbury Mountains, obviously exploring to see if a wagon road would be feasible. It wasn't.

Travel 0.5 miles west on Clark Street, just north of the museum, and turn right onto the Lincoln Highway (not the original, but a later version). For the next 3.0 miles this highway was probably built over the Hastings Road as it headed toward the northern tip of the Stansbury Mountains.

Rejoin SR 138 and continue north on SR 138 to the JUNCTION (9.5 miles) with I-80 at Exit 84 ("Grantsville").

Travel west on I-80 to EXIT 77 (7.0 miles) ("Rowley/Dugway"). Travel south on the Dugway road, an unnumbered paved road in Skull Valley.

Writing in the Utah guide, Dale Morgan related the interesting ety-
mology of the word dugway. "The word 'dugway' is of Mormon vintage,
coined originally to designate a species of road which consisted essentially of a deep rut scraped into the face of a hill. A wagon with its upper
wheels sunk to the hub in this rut, and with a spare team pulling uphill
to keep it from tipping, could 'go up, down, or around almost any hill
with a pitch less than 90 degrees.' " The word was applied later to any
road excavated around the side of a mountain or dug as a ramp down the
steep bank of a dry wash or a river.

Optional tour to view the Hastings Road. On the south side of I-80,
turn immediately into the large parking area, take the first dirt road to
the east, and travel 0.6 miles to Timpie Spring (salt) which is very near
I-80. View the Hastings Road on the east bank of the spring and continuing to the south-southwest. Note that a straight, gravel, automobile
road has obliterated almost any trace of the pioneer road; however, faint
traces of it may be found as it angles a bit to the right.
Return to paved highway.

Travel south on the Dugway road to BURNT SPRING (5.4 miles).
Just to the south of the abandoned ranch house, on the west side of the
road, the outlines and channels of the now-dry spring may be seen.
Frémont was here about 24 October 1845. From this point, he went
slightly south of due west twelve miles to Redlum Spring. On the far
hillside, just to the right of a ridge in the valley, a darker patch of trees
may be seen. This is the location of Redlum Spring. To the left (south)
of the spring is a low spot on the crest of the Cedar Mountains, an
apparent pass. This is the pass by which Frémont (1845) and Clyman and
Hastings (eastbound in May 1846) crossed the Cedar Mountains. T. H.
Jefferson and Lienhard also camped at Burnt Spring on 14 August 1846.
Stansbury's journal of 1849, describing his eastward travel over the Cedar
Mountains, clearly establishes these landmarks:

> Crossed the mountains through the pass [Hastings Pass] following the
> wagon road. It is about 5 miles north of where Fremont crossed.... After
> crossing continued down the east slope of the mountain for about two
> miles when we came to a spring [Redlum Spring] with some green grass
> growing in the water.... This was one of Fremonts camping grounds
> before crossing the mountain which he did through a pass at this place.
> From this spring our course lay about East across a broad valley of 10 miles
> wide.... Reaching the eastern mountain foot came to a Spring [Burnt
> Spring] where had been another Camping ground of Fremont.

Continue south on the Dugway road to HORSESHOE SPRING (4.0 miles). The old road may be seen adjacent to the spring and continuing on to the south over the slight rise.

Optional tour to Delle Ranch Spring. Delle Ranch Spring, called Cedar Spring on the T. H. Jefferson map, and located approximately 1.5 miles south of Horseshoe Spring and approximately 2.0 miles east up a ranch road, was a major gathering place during the gold rush. Delle Ranch Spring is worth visiting because it is a beautiful mountain spring and the view of the northern section of Skull Valley shows why Hastings had to lead the wagons so far south in order to gain passage across the valley. T. H. Jefferson described it: "North-east of Hope-Wells, upon the mountain, about two miles from the road, is situated Cedar Spring. It affords an abundant supply of delightful water, has cedar trees and some bunch grass near it; a horse trail leads to it from Hastings-Wells, over the mountain."
Return to the Dugway road.

Continue south on the Dugway road to SKULL VALLEY RANCH (IOSEPA) (5.8 miles). The several springs in the patches of cottonwood trees to the west of the highway were called "Hope Wells" by T. H. Jefferson and others of the 1846 emigration. The camping ground was located to the north of the spring and to the west of the highway. This was the last really good water and grass available before "The Fearful Long Drive" although some brackish water and limited grass were to be found at Redlum Spring twelve miles across the valley. This was where Tamsen Donner was able to piece together a note that had been left for them by Hastings which said "2 days-2 nights–hard driving–cross-desert–reach water." If you want to walk down to the spring, you should ask permission from any of the ranch employees you can find. Some of the Skull Valley Ranch buildings are the remains of the Hawaiian village of Iosepa (1889–1917). Just next to the first house on the east of the highway, a road leads to the Hawaiian cemetery and to the Hastings Road overlook on private property.

Optional tour to the Hastings Road overlook (private property). About 0.5 miles up this dirt road take the second road to the right, leading just south of east, for a total distance of 0.7 miles from the Dugway road. This is an excellent viewpoint to look northwest across Skull Valley to Hastings Pass (about N55°W by compass bearing), with the Hastings

Road clearly visible (with field glasses) extending up the far slope, slightly to the left of the pass. The cemetery may be seen one-half mile to the north.

Return to the Dugway road.

To follow the Hastings Road across Skull Valley and over Hastings Pass to Aragonite on the west side of the Cedar Mountains, *four-wheel drive vehicles are required and then only when the roads are not muddy* (the mud in the center of the valley can be sticky grease). During dry periods, passenger cars can often negotiate alternate roads other than the Hastings Road across the valley. However, these roads are infrequently graded, and since there are no culverts or bridges, travel to Redlum Spring can be problematical. Thus, any but ardent trail buffs are advised to return to I-80 and approach Hastings Pass from Exit 70 at Delle, following Route 4 as described below. Four alternate routes to Redlum Spring will be described: Hastings Road, Henry Spring road, Eightmile Spring road, and Hastings Pass road from Delle.

Continue south on the Dugway road to EIGHTMILE SPRING ROAD (1.6 miles). The first three of the routes are reached from the Eightmile Spring road junction, 1.6 miles south of the Skull Valley Ranch at Iosepa. This junction and Route 3 are shown on the state-issued "Utah Official Highway Map."

The junction of the Dugway road and Eightmile Spring road is the starting point to access the three routes described separately as follows. Set your odometer to 0.0 at this junction. The dirt road goes west and then northwest after approximately 1.4 miles.

Route 1. Hastings Road across Skull Valley. At 3.7 miles a dirt road angles off to the right. This ranch road then curves more to the right and proceeds north down the valley. The junction with the Hastings Road is 6.6 miles from the Dugway road. Note that this section of the Hastings Road, which runs northwest and southeast from this point, has been used as a ranch road. Follow the road to the northwest without making any major change in direction, although a few minor detours will be necessary. After a mile or two, the pioneer road will appear as an eroded ditch next to the ranch road. Lienhard's journal for 17 August 1846 says: "Before us lay a broad salt plain or valley, where grew only a very little thorny, stunted vegetation; indeed, the ground was often a salt crust. Our direction was northwesterly, in a straight line to the mountain opposite."

After about 2.0 miles there is no ranch road, and it is necessary to drive through the brush along the left side of the road.

At 11.6 miles is a major dry wash channel from Henry Spring gulch. At this point one branch of the road turned west and went up the gulch by a more direct route to Redlum Spring. This alternate trail, noted in some 1850 accounts, was made later than the major migrations since it had less traffic than the main road. The original road may be found on the north side of the wash as it heads toward Hastings Pass. Continue on to the northwest and observe this section of the road, which probably has not been used as a ranch road for well over a century.

At 12.4 miles the road is blocked by a BLM fence. Those wishing to walk the remaining pristine portion of the road will find that within about 1.0 miles it intersects the westside automobile road. Vehicles must turn west on the fence line road.

At 13.3 miles is the junction with the westside road. Turn right over the CATTLEGUARD.

Two alternate routes that reach this point are the Henry Spring road and the Eightmile Spring road. These two routes do not always require a four-wheel drive vehicle.

Route 2. Henry Spring road. Start from the Dugway road as above for the Hastings Road. At 4.3 miles is a fork near an excavated pit. Eightmile Spring road turns west. The less-traveled road heading northwest directly from the pit leads to Henry Spring.

At 11.4 miles is the junction with the westside road. Turn sharp right. Go 0.5 miles to the CATTLEGUARD at the fence line.

Caution: The road continuing to Henry Spring may be the more obvious one, but it goes west between the two distinctive north-south hills and should not be followed.

Route 3. Eightmile Spring road. Start from the Dugway road as above for the Hastings Road. At 4.3 miles is a fork near an excavated pit. Turn left and go straight west. At 8.5 miles is Eightmile Spring. Bear left and at the 0.1 miles intersection turn north along the hillside above the spring. Clyman and Hastings were here on 30 May 1846, on their way east. At the spring, find the road leading north and follow it, staying to the right of the north-south hills.

At 14.5 miles is the east-west fence and the CATTLEGUARD.

Routes 1, 2, and 3 (continued). Set your odometer to 0.0 at this point. Travel north from the east-west fence line and CATTLEGUARD. At

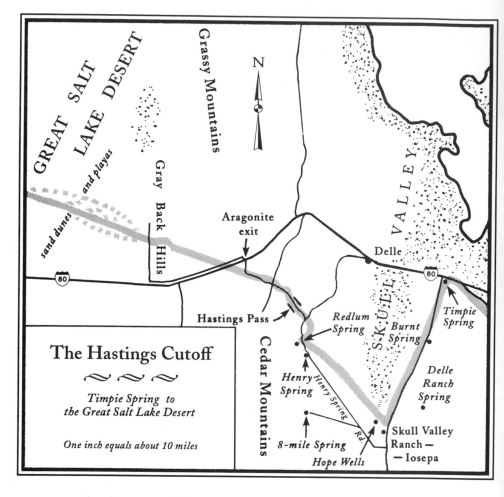

The Hastings Cutoff

～ ～ ～

*Timpie Spring to
the Great Salt Lake Desert*

One inch equals about 10 miles

0.9 miles the trace of Hastings Road comes from the right and becomes the alignment of the automobile road as it bends to the west. If any passengers on Route 1 decided to walk the Hastings Road after scrambling through the barbed-wire BLM fence, this is where to meet them.

Note the deep dry wash at 1.2 miles, just to the left of the automobile road. This is where the Hastings Road captured storm runoffs and was washed out. You can find some wagon tracks leading up to ten-foot-high dry wash banks. The automobile road is very close to the Hastings Road from here to the Redlum Spring dry stream channel.

At 2.0 miles is the Redlum Spring dry stream channel. Bryant's journal for 2 August 1846 says: "Descending into the plain or valley [Skull Valley] before us, we took a northwest course across it, striking Capt.

Fremont's trail of last year after we had commenced the ascent of the slope on the western side."

From here, look east across the valley to Burnt Spring. This is the course of Frémont's trail. If you then face west, you will note that the continuation of that line crosses the stream channel and goes up the hill. If you walk up the hill, you may find the pristine trace of the Hastings Road as it heads for Redlum Spring. The automobile road, however, turns southwest and follows up the stream bed for 1.0 miles, where it climbs a steep, gravel hill, on top of which you will cross the Hastings Road. In another hundred feet, you will meet the road from Hastings Pass. Turn sharp left at the junction and proceed 0.3 miles, staying on the right-hand branch. Park on the north side of the ravine.

REDLUM SPRING VIEWPOINT (3.3 miles). Redlum Spring is in the bottom of the ravine and issues from the south bank. The Bryant-Russell party camped here 2 August 1846, and the next day, guided by Hudspeth, went up Redlum Canyon. Lienhard's journal for 17 August 1846 says:

> After a time the road began to ascend a hill we reached a spring rather high on the mountainside . . . the water, although rather attractive to look at, was quite salty and the stock were not yet thirsty enough to drink it. Similarly, the small supply of coarse grass in no wise served, for they were not hungry enough to eat it.

Reverse your direction and follow the road 2.4 miles east and then north to the marked Hastings Pass junction. Observe dugways and swales of the pioneer road on both sides of the automobile road.

Route 4. Hastings Pass road from Delle. At the junction of I-80 and Exit 70 ("Delle"), follow the south side frontage road west for approximately 1.7 miles to where the road turns south. After another 9.2 miles over a rather rough and dusty road, which is suitable for passenger automobiles in dry weather, the junction with the road from Redlum Spring will be found.

Hastings Pass junction (eastside approach to Hastings Pass). Set your odometer to 0.0 at this point. At the Hastings Pass junction, the automobile road climbs a small hill before descending to enter the mouth of the canyon. Note that the eroded pioneer road is just to the south of the automobile road at the junction and then goes directly west up the dry wash into the mouth of the canyon. The two roads mostly coincide from here to near the top of the pass.

At 1.9 miles from the Hastings Pass junction a dirt road to the left is a section of the original Hastings Road. At 2.8 miles, where the automobile road is cut around a ridge on the left and commences its climb up a side-hill cut on the right flank of the canyon, the Hastings Road goes up that ridge on the left. This section of the Hastings Road is pristine and worth walking.

Continue to the HASTINGS PASS SUMMIT (3.4 miles).

Optional tour to the Skull Valley overlook. Take the dirt road south along the crest. In about one hundred yards you will find a good place to look back down into Skull Valley where you can see the trees at Hope Wells and the trace of the Hastings Road as it comes across the valley floor. Continue along the crest down a slight hill and then up a rather steep one for 0.3 miles from the main road. You will then be on top of the ridge up which the Hastings Road climbs from the east. Note that the Hastings Road goes down the last steep hill you have just come up and from the bottom drops on down into the gully on the west.

Return to the main Hastings Pass road and go west.

The road down the western side of Hastings Pass generally follows the trail of the pioneers. Near the bottom it passes an open-pit mining operation from which a white limestone rock is produced. After crossing a dry wash just beyond the mine, the present road swings left around a ridge at 2.8 miles. The Hastings Road, however, climbs over that ridge, and faint traces of the road may be found.

From the top of the ridge at the Hastings Pass west outlet, the pioneers had their first view of the dreaded passage ahead and of Pilot Peak if the atmosphere was clear enough. When Bryant reached the top of the Cedar Mountains on 3 August 1846, however, he couldn't see it. In his journal he says: "Here we should have had a view of the mountain at the foot of which our day's journey was to terminate, but for the dense smoke which hung over and filled the plain, shutting from the vision all distant objects." This severely limited visibility apparently continued over the next few weeks during which the 1846 emigrant wagon trains traveled.

Farther down the slope, the Hastings Road curves to the west, mostly along the present road, and heads directly toward Pilot Peak, but also due compass west. The Hastings Road went directly through the yard of the rock processing plant at the Aragonite railroad siding. From here on, over Grayback Hills and well out into the salt plain, the Hastings Road continues in a nearly straight line.

Follow the dirt road west for 2.0 miles, and then go north on the new paved road to the JUNCTION of I-80 and Exit 56 ("Aragonite"). Set your odometer to 0.0 at this point. Cross I-80 and turn left onto the northside frontage road. Follow the frontage road west up a slight rise and past the I-80 viewpoint before descending onto the valley floor.

Continue on the frontage road 3.5 miles to view where the Hastings Road crossed. The large highway sign ("View Area 1 Mile") on the eastbound lane of I-80 is approximately one hundred feet west of the Hastings Road. By placing yourself on a line between the sign and Pilot Peak, you will be able to see the trace of the Hastings Road as it approaches from Aragonite. Also, look to the west and note the low spot on the ridge of Grayback Hills with Pilot Peak visible in the distance. For the truly adventurous trail buff, that pass may be reached from here, but only with a four-wheel drive vehicle. The Hastings Road from here to Grayback Hills is not well defined enough to be followed on the ground; however, it usually can be seen clearly from a low-flying airplane.

Proceed west on the frontage road to the south end of Grayback Hills. At 9.0 miles you will reach the westernmost road that leads to a gravel pit on the hillside and adjacent to a north-south branch power line. When Frémont made his traverse from the Cedar Mountains to the north end of Silver Island, his trail passed the southern tip of Grayback Hills at this place. One-tenth of a mile to the north, an east-west power line had a service road along its north side. Travel west just to the right of the power line for 0.5 miles to find the northwesterly trending dirt road on the west side of Grayback Hills, and follow it to the north.

Continue northward on the dirt road to the HASTINGS ROAD (14.1 miles). Leading approximately 16° south of east (or just about due compass east) toward Grayback Hills are a set of tire tracks; that is, another dirt road which is mostly on top of the Hastings Road. Note that this is not quite as well traveled as the section-line road which is about one-quarter mile to the south. Follow these tracks about 1.0 miles and park at the edge of the hill.

Optional walking tour across Grayback Hills. One hundred eighty feet to the south will be found a rock cairn and a BLM section corner (Sections 25, 26, 35 & 36, TIN, R12W). If you have inadvertently followed the section-line road, it will lead you to this monument from which you can drive the 180 feet north to the Hastings Road. To the east on a magnetic, or compass, bearing of N75°E, at a distance of 430 feet is another rock cairn marking the location of the Hastings Road. The remains of the

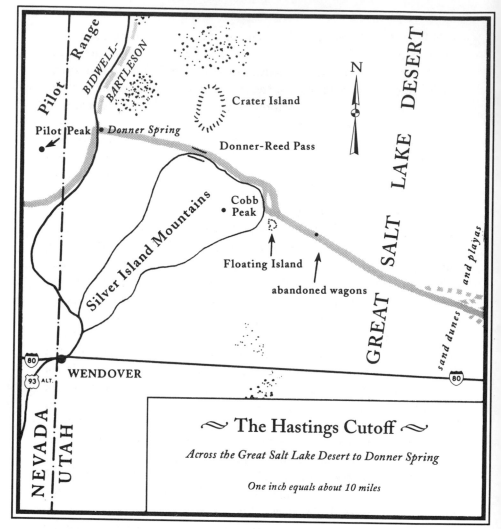

~ **The Hastings Cutoff** ~

Across the Great Salt Lake Desert to Donner Spring

One inch equals about 10 miles

road may be identified by wheel scratches on the volcanic boulders and a slight depression in the hillside. From here the road bends a bit more to the north on a bearing of N65°E for about 730 feet, passing a third rock cairn. It then curves more to the east on a bearing of N83°E for another 220 feet to another cairn and then continues on to the top of the hill and a bearing of S75°E.

The rock cairn near the top of the ridge marks a bend to the south in the Hastings Road onto a new bearing of S20°E. After four hundred feet, the Hastings Road descends the east slope of Grayback Hills on essentially the same bearing. The lack of boulders on this angling side-hill trace probably indicates that a side-hill cut (or dugway) was made and that the cut has filled in over the intervening years. The "narrow gap" with perpendicular walls, by which Bryant ascended Grayback Hills, is just 1.6 miles to the south along the ridge top and may be reached by a four-wheel drive road.

The Hastings Road to the west of Grayback Hills is marked approximately by a set of automobile tire tracks. These may be seen clearly from the summit of the ridge as they head generally toward Pilot Peak or compass west (approximately 16° north of true west). This dirt road, wandering from side to side of the Hastings Road, veers off to the right before reaching a World War II airstrip and may possibly follow one of the many detours established in later years. The original Hastings Road with only occasional faint traces remaining continued on west, wending its way through the playas and sand dunes until it connected with Frémont's trail and then headed toward Cobb Peak, as a landmark, on the northern end of Silver Island. Prior to 1986, when the sand dune and playa area was mostly undisturbed, a number of alternate tracks could be found. Since some of the playas become impassable after a rainstorm and several of the gold rush journals speak of rain, the detours would appear to be explained. The whole collection of tracks extending from here to Silver Island, rather than any single set, should be considered as the Hastings Road, even though traces of the original essentially straight path, as shown on T. H. Jefferson's map, were found and photographed in the 1970s.

The area to the west of Grayback Hills is no longer available for historical exploration, since it is now the site of both a hazardous waste dump and salt evaporation ponds.

Retrace your route back to the frontage road and travel west to enter I-80 at Exit 41 ("Knolls").

Travel west on I-80 to EXIT 4 (37.0 miles) ("Bonneville Speedway"). Travel north for 1.5 miles, then turn west onto the dirt road at the "TL Bar 23 Miles" sign. Continue for 0.8 miles, then turn sharp right onto the unmarked eastside Silver Island road.

Travel on the Silver Island road to the NORTHEAST TIP OF SILVER ISLAND (26.3 miles). This is where the Hastings Road came off the salt plain. Roughly two miles to the east lies Floating Island, which is about one-half mile south of the Hastings Road. Bryant's description is excellent:

About five o'clock, P.M., we reached and passed, leaving it to our left, a small butte rising solitary from the plain [Floating Island]. Around this the ground is uneven, and a few scattering shrubs, leafless and without verdure, raised themselves above the white sand and saline matter, which seemed recently to have drifted so as nearly to conceal them. Eight miles brought us to the northern end of a short range of mountains, turning the point of which and bending our course to the left, we gradually came upon higher ground, composed of compact volcanic gravel . . . . when I reached and turned the point . . . passing down the range of mountains on my left some four or five miles, and then rising some rocky hills connecting this with a long and high range of mountains on my right. . . . When I had reached the most elevated point of this ridge . . . I saw . . . a plain or valley of salt, some ten or twelve miles in breadth. On the opposite side of this valley rose abruptly and to a high elevation another mountain, at the foot of which we expected to find the spring of fresh water.

The remains of five wagons, which have often been noted, were located back along the trail at a distance of eight to ten miles. All traces of the wagon tracks on the salt plain near there have been covered by the thick new layer of salt deposited after this area was flooded in 1986 by the Great Salt Lake pumps.

Optional tour to wagon tracks viewpoint. As you approach Floating Island along the Silver Island road, you may note a somewhat obscure dirt road leading off to the northeast about eight miles to reach the north side of Floating Island. To the northeast, about 0.5 miles out on the salt, you may be able to find a set of wagon tracks leading to the tip of Silver Island. In 1990, one spot along these tracks was marked with a yellow stake.

Return to the Silver Island road.

Continue to DONNER PASS (6.4 miles). At this point the automobile road turns north but the Hastings Road continues in a straight line toward Donner Spring on the far side of the salt plain ahead. In about 0.6 miles at a junction turn sharp left and start south on the westside road.

Continue to DONNER SPRING AND WAGON TRACKS VIEWPOINT (1.4 miles). A small pile of rocks and a new trail marker identify where the Hastings Road crosses the automobile road. From here, the trace of the wagon road on the salt usually may be seen. Upon closer inspection, the faint remains of the Hastings Road through the sage on either side of the automobile road may be located. Lienhard reported the sight as follows:

The valley between us and the haze-shrouded mountains in the distance looked like a wide, large lake, the apparent surface of which here and there mirrored a deceptive semblance of the mountains and hills; we knew, however, that this was only a mirage, having already experienced several illusions of the kind. Straight through the seeming expanse of water from the opposite shore, a black monster moved toward us like a frightful, giant snake, in a long sinuous line. . . . as we travelled slowly down the hill . . . we realized that what we saw was neither a monstrous snake nor friendly Indians, but a considerable number of men with oxen, . . . who were going back into the barren desert to recover their abandoned wagons.

Warning: do not attempt to follow the Hastings Road across the salt plain. Instead, proceed down the unmarked westside Silver Island road.

Continue on the Silver Island road to the JUNCTION (18.6 miles) with the Donner Spring road ("TL Bar Ranch" sign). Turn west onto the Donner Spring road leading up the west side of the salt plain.

Travel north on the Donner Spring road to STEPHENS RANCH (19.4 miles). Drive into the Stephens Ranch, formerly the McKeller Ranch, and follow the signs north to Donner Spring. The series of springs along the eastern base of Pilot Peak were important for travelers across the Great Salt Lake Desert. First visited by the Bidwell-Bartleson emigrant party in 1841, the springs were visited by the Bryant-Russell, Harlan-Young, Hoppe-Lienhard, and Donner-Reed parties in 1846 after their respective crossings of the Great Salt Lake Desert. The Utah Crossroads chapter of the Oregon-California Trails Association has erected a fence around Donner Spring to protect its scenic and historical integrity. The fence and a planned interpretative sign are scheduled for dedication in August 1994, during the annual convention of the Oregon-California Trails Association in Salt Lake City.

T. H. Jefferson, traveling with the Hoppe-Lienhard party, described the "Long Drive":

Long Drive, Desert of Utariah. — Distance — From Hope-Wells to the East side of Scorpian Mt. [Cedar Mountains], 12 miles. Road good, a level plain. East to west side Scorpian Mt., 9 miles. Road, steep hills, some sideling, rather bad. West side Scorpian Mt., to Rock Ridge [Grayback Hills] 14 miles. Road good, hard marly plain.

Rock Ridge to east side Fire Mt. [Silver Island], 32 miles. Road a vast desert plain, good hard marl in places, deep sand ridges in places, latter part damp or wet marl incrusted with salt, into which the wheels cut and make hard pulling. From east to west side Fire Mt., 8 miles. Road hilly, deep dust, bunch grass in places, rather hard. From west side Fire Mt. to Bonark Wells [Donner Spring], 8 miles. Road a level plain of marl, damp, incrusted with fine table salt, rather hard pulling. Total distance 83 miles.

After visiting Donner Spring, turn around and travel south on the Donner Spring road, past the "TL Bar Ranch" sign, to I-80, EXIT 4 (24.0 miles). At this point you are 117 miles west of Salt Lake City and 3 miles east of the Utah-Nevada border.

Hensley's Salt Lake Cutoff

Will Bagley

City of Rocks, named for its monolithic rock formations. *Photograph by David E. Miller, from Photograph Archives, Utah State Historical Society.*

HISTORICAL PERSPECTIVE

On 9 April 1849, the *Warsaw Signal* of Illinois published a letter from Hazen Kimball, who wrote from California describing the events that set the stage for the opening of a viable wagon road from Salt Lake Valley to the California Trail.

> I arrived in the Salt Lake Valley on the 3rd of October, 1847, and remained there during the winter. On the 2nd of March, I left in company with one team for Fort Hall — a distance of 200 miles — where a wagon had never been before without a guide [and] without difficulty. On the 15th of July, I left Fort Hall with [James Clyman's party of] 25 wagons and 34 men, emigrants from the States to California. We had very good luck — came over the Sierra by a new route, one the Mormons opened this fall on their way to the Salt Lake. The road is very good — much better than the old one, it is said by those who have traveled both.

The existence of Fort Hall made it inevitable that the Mormons would open a wagon road between Great Salt Lake City and the Hudson's Bay Company trading post on the Snake River. Part of the road had originally been used by wagons in 1846, when Lansford W. Hastings brought the Harlan-Young party from the mouth of Weber Canyon to the future site of Salt Lake City. The discovery of the Salt Lake Cutoff was "a direct consequence of the shortcomings of the Hastings Cutoff as a means of access to the California Trail from the valley of the Great Salt Lake."

In the summer of 1848, adventurer Samuel J. Hensley, who seldom failed, "got defeated in attempting to take Hastings' Cut Off." Hensley was born in Kentucky in 1816 and worked as a trapper in New Mexico. He arrived in California with the 1843 Chiles party and worked for John Sutter. He was a prominent figure in the Bear Flag Revolt and served as a captain, and then major, in Frémont's California Battalion. Hensley returned to the states with Commodore R. F. Stockton's party in 1847 to testify at Frémont's court martial. In the spring of 1848, he headed west again with the pack train that opened the Salt Lake Cutoff. In California he became a merchant, Sam Brannan's banking partner, president of the California Steam Navigation Company, and a respected pioneer. "Major" Hensley helped secure a pension from the California legislature for famed trapper Thomas "Peg-leg" Smith, and supplied Smith with whiskey and tobacco while he was in the hospital. Hensley died at Warm Springs, Alameda County, California, on 7 January 1866. Hubert Howe Bancroft wrote that Hensley was "an honest and successful man of business, of strong will and well-balanced mind, generous, temperate, and brave."

On 17 August 1848, the diary of overlander Richard Martin May described one of the most significant events in Hensley's colorful life. On Goose Creek,

> Major Hensley who Left us at independence rock with the Mule Train overtook us to day. He intinded to pass to Fort Bridger & Thence South of Salt lake intending to follow [the Hastings Cutoff] Trail. He passed on without difficulty untill he Reached the South western portion of the Lake and Traveled Several Miles upon an incrustation of Salt and unfortunately for the Major and his Train (10 in number) There fell a heavy rain which So weakened the incrustation that they were verry near perishing in the mire. They were under the necessity of Cutting Loose the packs to Save the animals. in this way they lost their provision or nearly So with part of their clothing[.] They were 48 hours without food or water and hard at work most of the time to Save the Property[.] They then retraced their Steps to the Mormon City and there replenished their Larder[.]

May had earlier counted twelve men with Hensley, and at Goose Creek noted "that there was good mountainers & energetic men in that Little band."

On 9 August, the Mormon authorities in Great Salt Lake City reported to Brigham Young, then en route to the valley, that "Ten of the U.S. Troops under Capt. Hensley lately arrived in our valley on their way to California; they tried the Hastings route, but the desert was so miry from heavy rains that they have returned and gone on by way of Fort Hall." This letter was "perhaps erroneous" in one respect: the men with Hensley (as Dale Morgan wrote), "were more probably discharged troops than U.S. soldiers." The letter was certainly incorrect in one detail: Hensley would not go by way of Fort Hall.

Hensley did indeed head north, following Hazen Kimball's wagon tracks, but his party turned west after fording the Malad River to pioneer a new route. Ironically, none of Hensley's California biographers mentioned this incident, and it remained for historians J. Roderic Korns and Dale L. Morgan to reconstruct Hensley's pathfinding from Mormon sources. Hensley, of course, followed ancient Indian trails from spring to spring, but he won credit for the discovery of the Salt Lake Cutoff, opening a new route to the gold fields. Hensley's cutoff joined the California Trail in modern Idaho at the City of Rocks, near the present Utah-Nevada border.

Hensley proceeded to the Humboldt River, where on 27 August 1848, he met the Thompson company, a wagon train of discharged Mormon

Battalion veterans bound from Sutter's Fort to Salt Lake City. The party included diarists Henry Bigler, Azariah Smith, Addison Pratt, Jonathan Holmes, Samuel Rogers, and Ephraim Green. Hazen Kimball had met these men on 15 August, and they were the party he wrote had come "over the Sierra by a new route," opening the Carson Pass trail that became the main gateway to California in 1849. On one late August Sunday, the Mormons "laid by" for the day and had just concluded a prayer meeting when, as Henry Bigler's daybook describes it, Hensley's party entered their camp.

> [W]e was met by Capt. S. Hinsley [and] a packing company of 10 men[.] we got a way bill of our Road from here to salt lake and not [to] go by Ft Hall and save a bout 8 or 10 days travel. we learn from Mr. Hinsley that it is not more than a bout 380 miles to the lake [and] to take a serten cut off which we are sure to find with plenty of wood and water and grass [by] a route that he cum but waggons have never went there before[—]a good waggon rout[—]he got defeated in attempting to go Haistings cut off and turned back and found this knew rout of 70 miles saveing a bout 150 or 200 m.

Hensley's "way bill" described how to find his trail near the City of Rocks. On Thursday, 14 September, James Sly "found the turn off place," and the next day the company left the "Fort Hall road" and traveled about six miles, following Hensley's trail down Emigrant Canyon "through sage brush and over rocks and boulders." The Battalion veterans brought the first wagons over the cutoff. On the twenty-third, they found Hazen Kimball's wagon tracks, which they followed into the Utah settlements. Three of the diarists, Azariah Smith, Ephraim Green, and Samuel Rogers, recorded the distance between their camp on the upper Raft River and the Mormon settlement at Brownsville as 149, 151, and 150 miles, respectively.

Hensley's route, variously called the Salt Lake Cutoff, the Deep Creek Cutoff, and the Salt Lake Road, was only slightly shorter than the original (and easier) trail via Fort Hall. To paraphrase J. Goldsborough Bruff, the cutoff was not much of a cutoff at all. Nevertheless, the Salt Lake Cutoff provided a valuable link back to the California Trail for the estimated 25,000 overlanders in 1849 and 1850 who used the new Mormon settlement to recruit their animals and buy supplies. George R. Stewart estimated that one-third of all the overland forty-niners used the trail. The vanguard of the 1849 emigration, a pack-train party, reached Great Salt Lake City on June 16, and James C. Sly, a veteran of the Thompson company, led the first wagon party of forty-niners to the City of Rocks on 2 July 1849.

In the early 1850s, the Saints took active measures to promote the new route. At South Pass in 1852, Addison Crane met "a very good looking young man on a mule 6 days from Salt Lake — sent out as a runner to turn emigrants that way — he distributed a large hand bill setting forth the advantages of the route and promising good usage to all who should come to see them — signed by the Governor & other principal men — we shall see how well these promises be kept."

The Mormons developed ferries and bridges to cross the important rivers on the cutoff, and their economic importance is shown by the first item on Albert Carrington's 5 January 1856 summary of the actions of territorial legislature: "The Bear river ferry and Malad bridge have been placed under the control of Brigham Young, sen. and Joseph Young, sen., for the three years next ensuing."

The profits that the Youngs anticipated from the bridge and ferry vanished in 1857, when use of the Salt Lake Cutoff declined radically due to the Mormon War. Territorial relations had disintegrated to the point that President Buchanan dispatched federal troops to Utah, and the approach of Johnston's Army put a pox on overland travel via the City of the Saints. For example, a survey of 1852 journals shows that approximately one out of every six overland emigrants (including Oregonians) used the Salt Lake Cutoff, while in 1857 and 1858 almost no travelers followed the route. The trail revived in 1859, but by this time the Mormons themselves discouraged its use. Overlander Noah Brooks remembered that in 1859 "it was evident that our company was not longed for by the Saints. . . . The Saints took every opportunity to let us see that we were not welcome, and frequent thefts of cattle and horses at night, among our neighbors, warned us that it would be well to light out as soon as possible."

In 1859, Captain J. H. Simpson surveyed a road to the south of both the Great Salt Lake Desert and the Humboldt River that crossed the Great Basin to Carson Valley. Simpson's trail became the stage road known as "the direct desert route" and the Pony Express trail of 1860, and even saw "a little travel by overland emigrants." Although the Salt Lake Cutoff did not "fall into desuetude" after the completion of the transcontinental railroad, it ceased to be a main corridor for overland emigration. The route continued to serve as a highway for travelers and freighters bound north from Utah to Idaho, Oregon, and Montana, and parts of the trail saw substantial use even after the completion of the railroad in 1869. Today, US 89, I-15, and I-84 follow the trace of the old cutoff.

SALT LAKE CITY TO CITY OF ROCKS, IDAHO

As with most emigrant trails, the Salt Lake Cutoff developed numerous variants and detours over the years. This tour follows the line of the "Emigrant Road from California" shown on Captain Howard Stansbury's "Map of the Great Salt Lake and Adjacent Country in the Territory of Utah." This map presented the information that topographical engineer Stansbury had gathered during his surveys of 1849 and 1850. As the first map to show the cutoff, it is the most likely representation of the route of the 1848 Thompson company, and certainly shows the trail used in the great migrations of 1849 and 1850.

Trail buffs L. A. Fleming and A. R. Standing published the definitive study of the Salt Lake Cutoff in the summer 1965 issue of the *Utah Historical Quarterly*. Unfortunately, they occasionally identified later freight and stage variants as the main trail, especially in the area between Salt Lake City and Ogden. This guide references these variants, but does not describe them in detail.

From Salt Lake City to Strevell Junction (just north of the Idaho state line), the road is paved. From Strevell to Almo and the Emigrant Canyon wash, the route follows an improved gravel road that is easily passable in a passenger car. Emigrant Canyon requires a four-wheel drive vehicle, but an excellent gravel road passes through the City of Rocks to the junction of the Salt Lake Cutoff and the California Trail.

The Salt Lake Cutoff left the Oregon-California Trail west of Fort Bridger and followed the Pioneer Trail into Salt Lake Valley, but the cutoff did not achieve a unique identity until it left Salt Lake City.

The automobile tour starts at PIONEER PARK (300 South 300 West), west of downtown Salt Lake City. Pioneer Park is the site of the "Old Fort" the Mormon pioneers constructed in the fall of 1847. As a consequence of the scarcity of timber in the valley, only the east wall was built of logs, while the rest of the fort was made of adobe bricks. Veterans of the Mormon Battalion, who had served in New Mexico, and Sam Brannan, who had seen the technique used in California, recommended the use of adobe. The original fort, "built as a continuation of huts joined together in rectangular form," enclosed ten acres and had walls that were

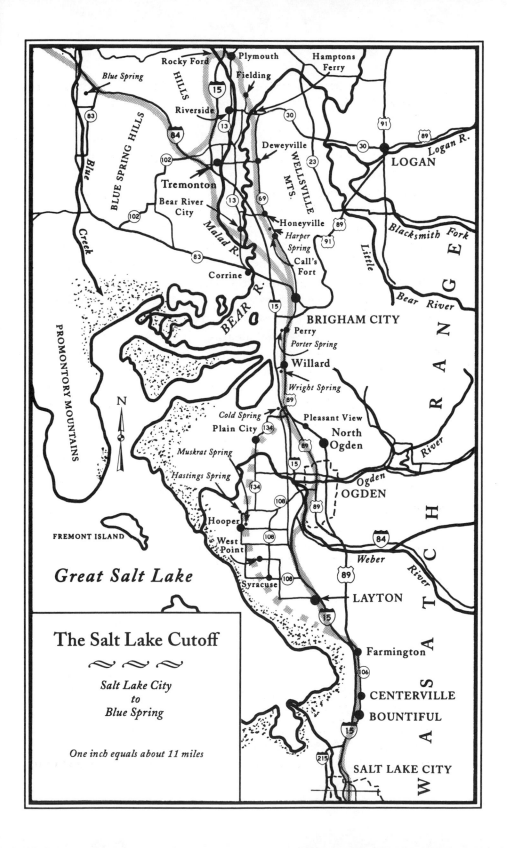

Blue Spring

HILLS

Rocky Ford   Plymouth   Hamptons
            Fielding   Ferry

15

Riverside

83

84

102

Deweyville

30

91

89

Logan R.

30

LOGAN

BLUE SPRING HILLS

Tremonton

Bear River
City

13

69

WELLSVILLE MTS.

23

Blacksmith Fork

102

83

Malad R.

Honeyville

Harper
Spring

Call's
Fort

89

91

Little

83

Corrine

BEAR R.

15

Bear   River

RANGE

BRIGHAM CITY

Perry

Porter Spring

PROMONTORY MOUNTAINS

Willard

Wright Spring

89

N

Cold Spring   Pleasant View

Plain City   134   North
                    Ogden

89

Muskrat Spring

15

River

Hastings Spring

134

Ogden

106   OGDEN

FREMONT ISLAND

Hooper

West
Point

108

89

Weber

84

River

Great Salt Lake

Syracuse

106

89

LAYTON

15

Farmington

106

The Salt Lake Cutoff

CENTERVILLE

BOUNTIFUL

15

Salt Lake City
to
Blue Spring

215

SALT LAKE CITY

One inch equals about 11 miles

WASATCH

twenty-seven inches thick and nine feet high. The compound was immediately expanded with two extensions known as the South Fort and North Fort. Most forty-niners passing through Great Salt Lake City camped at the site, and 1850 emigrant George Shepard reported that he "encampt at the old fort and put our horses in a pasture at fifteen cents a head pr twenty four hours." The structure did not stand up well to the elements, and had outlived its usefulness when the city council ordered its crumbling walls torn down in 1851.

The road running along the east edge of the park is 300 West. Travel north on 300 West to 600 North and the CHILDREN'S MUSEUM OF UTAH (1.8 miles). The museum is located upon the site of a hot spring and popular pioneer bath. Originally, the numerous springs in this area drained into two-mile-long Hot Springs Lake. Geothermal wonders dotted the landscape where the Wasatch Front met Great Salt Lake, and virtually every source account mentions the extraordinary mix of hot, warm, cold, and sulfur springs. Travelers used the springs for that rare overland luxury, a bath. Many of the springs were developed as health resorts in the late nineteenth century, but not one of these resorts survives.

Continue north on 300 West, which becomes US 89, to the JUNCTION (2.4 miles) with I-15. Enter I-15 and travel north. (The original trail generally follows the line of US 89, which can be reached via the North Salt Lake exit. Note, however, that the following mileages are based on traveling on I-15.) The "Hot Sulpher Spring," which 1859 emigrant Melyer Casler found "was so hot that I could not hold my hand in it a second," was located in the present town of Bountiful. The line of the old trail went through Bountiful and Centerville, site of an old Mormon fort and several historic homes built using its stones. On its way to Farmington, US 89 passes a number of well-preserved pioneer homes built of adobe and brick. Describing this "beautiful country" in August 1846, Heinrich Lienhard commented on the "fine road," which was only days-old at the time. Nothing remains of the trail in this heavily developed area.

Continue north on I-15 to FARMINGTON (12.6 miles). From Farmington, called Haight Creek or Halfway House by the first travelers and later Miller's Settlement, the original trail followed the high ground traversed by US 89 through modern Kaysville, Layton, and Clearfield to a Weber River ford about four miles below the site of mountain man Miles Goodyear's Fort Buenaventura. By May 1850, the Mormons had bridged the fords of both the Weber and Ogden rivers with limited success, as recounted in the journal of Louisa Pratt: "We found the Weber very high, the water running over the middle of the bridge. We got safely over, called at Brown's Fort. . . . We came to Ogden River, had an almost perpendicular hill to come down; the men let the wagons down by the help of ropes; had a severe time crossing the water. After we crossed the bridge, the wagons mired; the men were in the water up to their waists for more than an hour. . . . We heard afterwards the Weber bridge washed away the night after we crossed over." Until 1850, the Mormon settlement was known as Brown's Fort or Brownsville, after Captain James Brown of the Mormon Battalion, who used his men's back pay to purchase Utah's first white settlement from Goodyear in November 1847.

The original trail required fording both the Weber and Ogden rivers, and had to contend with "almost perpendicular" sandhills. As the country grew more settled, Noah Brooks reported, "to reach the road to Bear River, we were obliged to cross a few fenced fields, and this involved long parleys with surly owners." To avoid these problems, later variants of the cutoff swung to the west of Ogden along modern Bluff Road, made a single crossing of the Weber below its junction with the Ogden, and rejoined present US 89 northwest of Pleasant View near the Utah Hot Spring.

Continue north on I-15 to UNION STATION (21.1 miles), Ogden. From I-15, take Exit 344A and go left on Wall Avenue (which is also US 89). The best way to find Fort Buenaventura, now wonderfully restored as a Utah state park, is to ask directions at the Union Station Visitor's Center on Wall and 25th streets in historic downtown Ogden. (The fort is directly west across the railroad tracks from Union Station; to reach it go north on Wall to 24th Street, go west across the viaduct, and take the first left past a baseball diamond.) One of the most remarkable artifacts of the fur trade is Miles Goodyear's hewn-log cabin, now preserved at the Daughters of Utah Pioneers Museum at 2148 Grant Avenue.

From Ogden, follow US 89 north 6.0 miles to Pleasant View. Trail campsites can be traced by following the locations of springs. Perhaps the most important were the Utah Hot and Cold springs, located about a mile apart near the Weber-Box Elder county line. (From I-15, take Exit 354.) The hot springs are found below the present Rocky Point restaurant; as in 1859, the water "is clear, has a salty taste, and nothing grows where it runs off in the valley; it leaves a deposit like iron-rust." Cold Spring, also known as Marsh Spring, is 0.8 miles up US 89 from the Hot Springs. The town of Willard, named in 1857 for Willard Richards, counselor to Brigham Young, lies 6.1 miles north of Cold Spring. Wright Spring is 1.3 miles further north, under the willows visible to the west of the highway. About 2.0 miles further north is the hamlet of Perry, formerly known as Porter Spring, located west of the highway at the north end of Perry.

Continue north on US 89 to the TABERNACLE (21.0 miles), Brigham City. The trail rolled north through Box Elder, now Brigham City, keeping to the line of US 89. In 1859, Noah Brooks reported, "Box Elder was a settlement of about three hundred people, and boasted a post-office, a blacksmiths shop, a trading post, and a brewery." Leaving the town, the trail took to the high ground east of present SR 69 to avoid the wetlands around now-drained Box Elder Lake. This marshy ground was home to uncounted wildfowl in pioneer times. In 1848, John Borrowman described traveling "through a beautiful valley with a great many springs in it and some of them boiling hot and a large lake of fresh water is in this valley[.] we camped by a beautiful little stream with a grove of cottonwood by it." The trail ran slightly east of the present Main Street. At 2.1 miles north of the Brigham City Tabernacle, the trail passed through Cotter Farm, the white house visible east of the road.

From Brigham City, travel north on SR 69 to CALL'S FORT (7.7 miles). Call's Fort Historical Monument marks the site of a stone fort built in 1854 by Anson V. Call. North of Brigham City, the trail leaves existing roads behind and presents several touring options. The original trail left the line of the highway near Call's Fort and turned west to ford Bear River, "just above where Bear River City is now located," according to 1848 trail veteran James S. Brown.

Continue north on SR 69 to HONEYVILLE (2.3 miles). To follow the approximate original trail, take SR 69 into Honeyville. At the junction in town, turn onto SR 240 and travel west on SR 240 to the BEAR RIVER CROSSING (2.2 miles). The ford originally used by the Thompson company in 1848 was probably a short distance south of the point where 240 crosses the Bear. The Stansbury map, the most accurate representation of the trail in 1849 and 1850, shows that the trail forded the Bear River directly east of present Tremonton, and then turned southwest for 1.5 miles to cross the narrow but steep-banked Malad River.

Among the Thompson party journalists (who called the Malad "moody," "mudy," and "Muddy Crick"), Henry Bigler recorded the distance between the Malad and Bear rivers at seven miles; Holmes and

Green noted six miles; while Rogers and Smith gave the distance as four miles. The contradiction between the Thompson company journals and the Stansbury map indicates that by 1850, the Mormons had established better crossings, and makes positive identification of the original fords purely conjectural. At any rate, the Malad ford gave the 1848 Thompson company considerable grief. Henry Bigler wrote, "This morning in crossing the Malad we broke down a wagon. The crossing was very bad. The stream was narrow, not very deep, but the bottom very soft and muddy." Addison Pratt noted, "this was the worst creek to cross of any we found on the road, on account of its banks being muddy and the water near up to the waggon beds. Ours got over safe, but some others filled with water or capsized." The situation had not improved much by 1850, when Louisa Pratt called the crossing "one of the most intolerable place[s] my eyes ever beheld! Cattle and men up to their backs in mud."

To see the terrain that made the Malad River crossing so difficult, continue 0.5 miles from the Bear on SR 240 to the first junction and go south towards Bear River City. (Three-tenths of a mile down the road is a historical marker commemorating Jim Bridger's discovery of Great Salt Lake.) Turn west 0.7 miles further on at 6400 North and go 2.1 miles to the Malad.

To return to I-15, retrace your route, or go north on the county roads to TREMONTON (5.0 miles). The county road just north of Cropley junction crosses the Malad River again near the ruins of an early twentieth-century bridge that is probably on the site of one of the toll-bridges the Mormons built during the heyday of the Salt Lake Cutoff.

Optional tour to Boise Ford and Hampton Ferry. Many travelers sought to avoid the tolls the Mormons charged to cross the Malad and Bear rivers, including Noah Brooks: "At the crossing of the Bear River the ferryman demanded three dollars for each team carried across the river, the cattle being swum over even at that price. We went on ten miles up the river [to Hampton Ford], where we found a good crossing and saved our money." These trail variants made a looping detour to the north that required crossing the Bear River at either BOISE FORD, named because the Boise stage line used this crossing, or HAMPTON FORD, named after Ben Hampton. (A marker reading "Boise Ford, 1853" marks the site of the lower ford, but the marker was actually placed by the Boy Scouts sometime before 1965.) Ben Hampton and William S. Godbe established a ferry at Hampton Ford in 1853. Hampton and Godbe bridged the Bear in 1859, and received a territorial charter to rebuild it in 1866. The stone house now at the site was built in this same year and was known as the Bear River Hotel. The barn near the bridge was built shortly after the stone house. In 1875 the property passed to the Standing family, and in 1894 Jacob and Agnes Standing Bigler inherited the estate.

To explore this trail variant, turn east onto SR 102 in Tremonton and travel 2.6 miles to the junction with SR 69. Travel north 5.0 miles on SR 69 and take the left fork towards Riverside. At 0.6 miles, turn north onto 3400 West and travel 0.5 miles to the now-closed bridge at Hampton Ferry. Several old barns, including one that is now used as a dinner theater, recall the site's origins.

To cross the Malad River, some travelers followed the Bidwell–Bartleson route north to Rocky Ford, and then turned south to rejoin the trail at present-day Tremonton.

To visit Rocky Ford, return 0.5 miles to the main east-west road. Turn right onto this road and travel 2.5 miles to the junction with SR 13 at Riverside. Turn right onto SR 13 and travel 5.0 miles to the junction with a road on the left. A sign reading "Belmont Springs" is at this junction. To continue to Rocky Ford, follow the directions in the "Bidwell-Bartleson Trail" chapter.

Return to Tremonton.

From Tremonton, there is no avoiding I-84, which follows the track of the trail as it rounds Point Lookout and passes Blind Spring, before crossing the Blue Spring Hills to Blue Spring.

Travel west on I-84 to BLUE SPRING (16.9 miles). This spring was the worst watering hole on the Salt Lake Cutoff. Addison Pratt noted, "The water has a brackish sulphery taste and smell, and was the only bad water we camped on between the sink of Mary's River and Salt Lake." Gold rushers found the water so bad they could not even make drinkable tea out of it. Like all water resources in this arid country, the spring has been considerably developed since pioneer times and the water in the reservoir is now quite potable. To view the reservoir now created by the spring, take the Valley Exit 24 and go straight south 0.4 miles on the gravel road. Turn east at the crossroads and go 0.5 miles.

Continue west on I-84 to WARD RANCH (6.0 miles). Following the line of I-84, the trail crossed the North Promontory Mountains through Rattlesnake Pass into Hansel Valley, where it rounded Franklin Hill to reach Hansel's Spring, now Dillie Spring at Ward Ranch, which is located on private property. The trail crossed the foothills at the north end of the Hansel Mountains. The "Hansel" Mountains, Peak, Spring, and Valley are misnamed after S. J. Hensley, a process that began in 1851 with the publication of the *Mormon way bill, to the gold mines* of Joseph Cain and Arieh C. Brower, which referred to "Hensell's Spring." As J. Roderic Korns and Dale Morgan noted more than forty years ago, "Utah has repaid its debt to [Hensley] shabbily by corrupting his very name as it stands on the map. A poor memorial is better than none, [but] our maps should now be corrected."

Continue west to EXIT 5 (8.0 miles) ("Snowville"). I-84 follows the course of the cutoff to Snowville, where the trail encountered a substantial obstacle at Deep Creek. Azariah Smith's diary entry for 19 Septem-

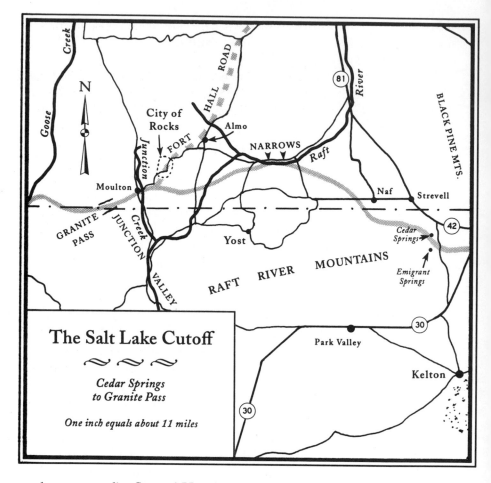

N

City of
Rocks

Almo

NARROWS

Moulton

Naf

Strevell

GRANITE
PASS

Yost

Cedar
Springs

42

RAFT RIVER MOUNTAINS

Emigrant
Springs

30

Park Valley

Kelton

The Salt Lake Cutoff

~ ~ ~

*Cedar Springs
to Granite Pass*

One inch equals about 11 miles

30

ber 1848 credits Samuel Hensley with naming the watercourse, and indicates Hensley constructed some sort of bridge to cross the ravine. This ford was probably located at a big bend about one mile west of Snowville.

Leaving I-84 3.0 miles west of Snowville near the present Rose Ranch, the trail parallels the course of SR 30/42 about one mile to the south as the road runs directly west across Curlew Valley. A gated dirt road 17.0 miles west of Snowville provides access to Pilot Spring. To reach the spring, go south 0.9 miles. Here a road turns southwest and runs 0.8 miles to Pilot Spring. Although the spring has been developed, excellent trail ruts can be found to both the east and west. In 1849, travelers could expect to find "2 lone springs in a desert place, with little or no grass." (Some emigrant journals called this Double Springs.) At CURLEW JUNCTION (18.4 miles), SR 30 goes south to Park Valley, following the route of the Boise-Kelton stage line, while SR 42 continues north into Idaho.

Optional tour to the Salt Lake Cutoff overlook. From Pilot Spring, the original trail went directly west 5.75 miles to Emigrant Spring. (A later variant went directly to Cedar Spring, two miles further north.) Near here, the 1848 Thompson party had its first view of Great Salt Lake. Emigrant Spring is on private property and is inaccessible, but the view from SR 30 is worth a short detour. To view the old trail, turn south on SR 30 to Park Valley at Curlew Junction and proceed 2.1 miles southwest to the point where the trail crosses the road. The elevation gives a spectacular view of the old trail looking east to Pilot Spring.
Return to SR 42.

Continue northwest on SR 42 to the IDAHO STATE LINE (8.3 miles). SR 42 crosses into Idaho.

Continue to STREVELL JUNCTION (1.3 miles). Here the road leaves SR 42 and pavement: the rest of the trip is on improved gravel county roads or four-wheel drive vehicle trails. The ruins and foundations just south of the junction are all that is left of Strevell. A sign on the highway points to National Forest Access. Turn west onto the county road.

Travel west on the county road to CLEAR CREEK ROAD (3.7 miles). In 1848, the Thompson company camped at the mouth of Clear Creek Canyon, which is several miles south up this road. Addison Pratt, an avid fisherman, reported, "I concluded there must be trout in it higher up where there was a running stream. After our camping affairs were arranged, I took my rifle, and steered off towards the head of the stream and soon obtained a goodly string and returned to camp with my fish, to the astonishment of all hands, and they gave it as a general opinion, that I could catch a mess of trout, if I could only find rainwater standing in a cow track." The road crosses Clear Creek approximately 0.5 miles east of Naf.

Continue west on the county road to NAF (0.7 miles). Pat's Mercantile and Cafe has gas, beer, and food, and is the last available refueling point on the road. (Pat's pre-inflation gas pump only has two digits.) The Salt Lake Cutoff trail crosses the county road 1.1 miles to the west of the Naf store, where extremely well-preserved ruts are visible just north of the road. From Naf, follow the highway signs to City of Rocks. About 7.0 miles west of Naf, the road forks. Take the right fork and proceed north. A sign reading "City of Rocks 17" points the way. About 5.0 miles further on, you'll reach a junction on the Raft River. Again, follow the road sign to City of Rocks, going west along the river.

Continue west along the river to the ranch house at the RAFT RIVER NARROWS (13.8 miles). The Narrows offers a great view of the Bookend Rocks, two deep-red mountains that 1848 emigrant John Borrowman called the "Two Sisters," not to be confused with the rock formation at the City of Rocks that Henry Bigler informs us was named the "Twin Sisters" by Addison Pratt. At the narrows, Pratt noted that "the stream was large and afforded plenty of trout." As you emerge from the narrows, the mouth of Emigrant Canyon (called Emigration Canyon on some maps) lies directly to the west-south-west. It is the lowest gap on the western horizon. The City of Rocks lies across the Raft River valley, just to the north of Emigrant Canyon. Cross the river at the next junction, following the sign to Almo and City of Rocks.

From this point, several carsonite Oregon-California Trails Association markers showing the location of the trail are visible from the road. Note the SALT LAKE CUTOFF MARKER (0.7 miles). The trail proceeded in a direct line for the mouth of Emigrant Canyon. The modern road crosses the valley at right angles, only occasionally crossing the trail.

Follow the county road west across the valley to the ALMO ROAD (7.6 miles). Turn south at the junction with the county road running north-south. As the junction is only 1.0 miles south of Almo, it is worth a trip into this charming hamlet to visit the National Park Service station, which has a wealth of free information available and a most helpful staff. Two-wheel drive vehicles should proceed to City of Rocks via Almo; four-wheel drive vehicles can proceed south to Emigrant Canyon.

The trail crosses the road at the SALT LAKE CUTOFF MARKER (3.3 miles). The City of Rocks is directly west. Continue south on the road a short distance to Emigrant Canyon Creek. Here the road crosses the dry wash that issues from Emigrant Canyon. Immediately south of the wash is a fence and a cattle guard across the road. Turn west onto the unimproved road and follow the fence line west. At the fork of the road 0.7 miles on, turn south at the open gate. The road turns west, heading towards the mouth of the canyon. It goes through an open fence gate with six large cedar posts.

The trail again crosses the road at the SALT LAKE CUTOFF MARKER (2.4 miles).

A Salt Lake Cutoff marker and a City of Rocks National Reserve sign mark the mouth of EMIGRANT CANYON (0.5 miles). Emigrant Canyon is the only section of the tour that requires four-wheel drive, and the road can be quite rough. (Total distance from gravel county road to county road is 4.9 miles.) A two-wheel drive truck with high clearance could reasonably negotiate the road, but it is definitely not recommended for passenger cars. The road often parallels the old wagon trail and stage route.

Travel 0.6 miles up the canyon where a wash enters from the north. Take the left fork. After another 0.6 miles, the road forks. Cross the wash of Emigrant Canyon Creek to the south side and follow the road as it goes west, or proceed west 0.1 miles to the ruins of a stage station on the Kelton-Boise road. Two log barns and a log station house with sod roofs survive at the station.

The trail connects with the county road at the head of EMIGRANT CANYON (1.9 miles). The Emigrant Canyon road is marked with a sign at the roadhead; a few yards before the end of the road is a barbed wire cattle fence gate. Make sure to close the gate.

Hensley's Salt Lake Cutoff meets the California Trail about forty yards south of the yellow TRAILS WEST MARKER (0.4 miles) on the county road. Standing directly north of the trail, two "towering rocks near each other," the Twin Sisters, provide an unmistakable landmark from the meadow below.

A visit to the City of Rocks, about 1.0 miles up the California Trail via Pinnacle Pass, provides an excellent end to the tour. Camping is available on a first-come basis, and information is available at the ranger station at Almo, about 4 miles up the California Trail from the junction.

City of Rocks is located in south-central Idaho, directly east of the meeting point of the Utah, Idaho, and Nevada borders. At this point you are 175 miles northwest of Salt Lake City.

Selected Bibliography

Harold Schindler

～

This brief supplemental list of books and articles on the Oregon and California trails is intended only as a guide to assist the general reader in gaining a perspective of the history of overland travel during those early decades of the 1800s. Incomplete and fragmentary, it is but a selected bibliography, and at best we risk being presumptuous in preparing even a short list for those who would learn more of the exploration and emigration through Utah. Readers may find some of these books more readily available in later editions. The compiler freely confesses to shamelessly borrowing from the scholarship of Ramon F. Adams, Robert E. Cowan, J. Frank Dobie, Lannon W. Mintz, Henry R. Wagner, Charles L. Camp, and the dean of western historians, Dale L. Morgan.

Allen, A. J. *Ten Years in Oregon; Travels and Adventures of Doctor E. White and Lady, West of the Rocky Mountains.* Ithaca: Mack, Andrus, & Co., 1848.
From Independence, 15 May 1842, with Medorem Crawford and L. W. Hastings. Hired Thomas Fitzpatrick at Fort Laramie as a guide to Fort Hall.

Alter, J. Cecil. *Jim Bridger.* Norman: University of Oklahoma Press, 1962.
The author, first director of the Utah State Historical Society, has here written the best biography of "Old Gabe" to be found.

Auerbach, Herbert S., ed. "Father Escalante's Journal with Related Documents and Maps." *Utah Historical Quarterly* 11 (1943).
The most important features of this scarce volume are the many old maps showing Spanish concepts of Lake Timpanogos and Rio de San Buenaventura, the early "Freiberg" map of the far West (about 1838), which shows Great Salt Lake as Timpanogos Lake, and a John Senex map (1810) with Baron LaHontan's earliest of all references to Great Salt Lake in 1689.

Bagley, Will, ed. *A Road from El Dorado: The 1848 Trail Journal of Ephraim Green*. Salt Lake City: Prairie Dog Press, 1991.
An eyewitness account of the opening of the first wagon road over Carson Pass in the summer of 1848. Valuable source on the movements of the elusive Samuel J. Hensley and the fabled mountaineer Joseph Reddeford Walker.

————, ed. *Frontiersman: Abner Blackburn's Narrative*. Salt Lake City: University of Utah Press, 1992.
Excellent treatment of the peregrinations of this Mormon memoir ranging from the troubles at Haun's Mill in Missouri to Nevada and the gold fields of California.

Barry, Louise. *The Beginning of the West: Annals of the Kansas Gateway to the American West, 1540–1854*. Topeka: Kansas State Historical Society, 1972.
This is a marvelously useful and informative reference source on overland travel. A monumental compilation that continues to influence scholarship concerning the American West.

Bigler, David L., ed. *The Gold Discovery Journal of Azariah Smith*. Salt Lake City: University of Utah Press, 1990.
One of the two men at the scene of the gold discovery at Sutter's Mill on 24 January 1848 who wrote of their experiences in personal diaries. Smith was a member of the company that opened the Mormon-Carson Pass Emigrant Trail over the Sierra Nevada to become a major route of the gold rush.

Brooks, George R., ed. *The Southwest Expedition of Jedediah S. Smith: His Personal Account of the Journey to California, 1826–1827*. Glendale: Arthur H. Clark, 1977.
A first-person account, astonishingly, by the first American to make the overland trip to California. The route follows from present Soda Springs to Utah Lake, Salina, St. George, to Needles, Los Angeles, to Sacramento, across the Sierra and present Nevada, to Great Salt Lake and Bear Lake. Much of the footnote material is Dale L. Morgan's scholarship.

Brown, James S. *Life of a Pioneer: Being the Autobiography of James S. Brown*. Salt Lake City: George Q. Cannon & Sons, 1900.
Left Nauvoo, joined the Mormon Battalion in its march overland to California. Participant in the discovery of gold at Sutter's Mill.

Brown, John. *Autobiography of Pioneer John Brown 1820–1896*. Arranged and published by his son, John Zimmerman Brown. Salt Lake City: Privately Printed, 1941.

Excellent account of the pioneer Mormon who led Mississippi Saints to Pueblo, Colorado, and, joining with the sick detachment of the Mormon Battalion, arrived in Great Salt Lake Valley at the same time as the main body of Mormon pioneers.

Bruff, J. Goldsborough. *Gold Rush: The Journals, Drawings, and other Papers of J. G. Bruff, Captain, Washington City and California Mining Association, 1849–1851.* Ed. by G. W. Read and R. Gaines. 2 vols. New York: Columbia University Press, 1944.
A draftsman in the U.S. Bureau of Topographical Engineers, Bruff organized a party of sixty-six for California by the Overland Trail. This is among the best of the gold rush accounts.

Bryant, Edwin. *What I Saw In California: Being the Journal of a Tour, by the Emigrant Route and South Pass of the Rocky Mountains, across the Continent of North America, the Great Desert Basin, and through California, in the Years 1846, 1847.* New York: D. Appleton & Co, 1848.
Praised as one of the most informative and readable records left by the overland travelers of 1846 or any other year, Bryant's book was published while most of the figures named in it were still alive. No casual accident, this book was planned by its author from the beginning; hence his careful attention to detail.

Campbell, Albert H. *Pacific Wagon Roads. Letter from the Secretary of the Interior, Transmitting a Report upon the Several Wagon Roads Constructed under the Direction of the Interior Department [Report by Albert H. Campbell, Dated 19 February 1859].* 35th Congress, 2nd Session, H.R. Executive Document No. 108 and Senate Executive Document No. 36. Washington, D.C.: Government Printing Office, 1859.
Important not only for fine field maps, but for various reports from superintendents under the Gen. Supt. Campbell. Includes emigrant guide from Gilbert Station at South Pass to California.

Clayton, William. *William Clayton's Journal: A Daily Record of the Journey of the Original Company of "Mormon" Pioneers from Nauvoo, Illinois, to the Valley of the Great Salt Lake.* Published by the Clayton Family Association. Salt Lake City: The Deseret News, 1921.
This famous journal needs no further comment.

Cline, Gloria Griffen. *Exploring the Great Basin.* Norman: University of Oklahoma, Press, 1963.
Handy reference for the Great Basin, "corridor to California."

Crampton, C. Gregory, and Steven K. Madsen. *In Search of the Spanish Trail; Santa Fe to Los Angeles, 1829–1848*. Layton: Gibbs M. Smith, Publisher, 1994.
This volume is the first-ever delineation-description of the Spanish Trail. The authors map the trail for the first time.

Crampton, C. Gregory. "Utah's Spanish Trail." *Utah Historical Quarterly* 47 (Fall 1979): 361–83.
One of Utah's experts on the Spanish Trail outlines this 1,120-mile trade route from Santa Fe to Los Angeles through Utah.

Fisher, Vardis, ed. *Idaho: A Guide in Word and Picture*. Caldwell: Caxton Printers, Ltd., 1937.
This was the first volume of the American Guide Series to be completed from among the many commissioned, thus it set the style for other state volumes yet to come.

Fleming, L. A., and A. R. Standing. "The Road to 'Fortune': The Salt Lake Cutoff." *Utah Historical Quarterly* 33 (Summer 1965): 248–71.
This article quotes from Korns's "West From Fort Bridger" in discussing Samuel J. Hensley's role in opening the Salt Lake Cutoff, but goes on to detail the development of the cutoff from 1849 through the mid-1860s.

Hafen, LeRoy R., and Ann W. Hafen. *Handcarts to Zion: The Story of a Unique Western Migration, 1856–1860, with Contemporary Journals, Accounts, Reports and Rosters of the Ten Handcart Companies*. Glendale: Arthur H. Clark, 1960.
The mass migration of the Mormon handcart companies was the most remarkable travel experiment in the history of the West.

————. *Journals of Forty-Niners, Salt Lake to Los Angeles: With Diaries and Contemporary Records of Sheldon Young, James S. Brown, Jacob Y. Stover, Charles C. Rich, Addison Pratt, Howard Egan, Henry W. Bigler, and Others*. Vol. 2. Far West and Rockies Series. Glendale: Arthur H. Clark, 1954.

————. *Old Spanish Trail, Santa Fe to Los Angeles: With Extracts from Contemporary Records and Including Diaries of Antonio Armijo and Orville Pratt*. Vol. 1. Far West and Rockies Series. Glendale: Arthur H. Clark, 1954.

Hafen, LeRoy R., and Francis Marion Young. *Fort Laramie and the Pageant of the West, 1834–1890*. Glendale: Arthur H. Clark, 1938.

History of fur trade, military on the frontier, and emigrants on the overland trail.

Hannon, Jessie Gould. *The Boston-Newton Company Venture: From Massachusetts to California in 1849*. Lincoln: University of Nebraska Press, 1969.
This group of goldseekers entered Great Salt Lake City on 7 August 1849, sold their wagons and bought pack saddles, opting to complete the journey with pack mules. Took the Salt Lake Cutoff pioneered the year before "by Samuel J. Hensley, returning to California from Washington, D. C." This volume brings together companion diaries kept by two members of the company Charles Gould and David Jackson Staples.

Hawkins, Bruce R., and David B. Madsen. *Excavation of the Donner-Reed Wagons: Historic Archaeology along the Hastings Cutoff.* With contributions by Ann Hanniball, Brigham D. Madsen, M. Elizabeth Manion, Gary Topping. Salt Lake City: University of Utah Press, 1990.
Sketchy overview of overland emigration, the California Trail, and the Hastings Cutoff as an introduction to detailed reports on previous expeditions to the abandoned wagon sites, excavation procedures and discoveries. All a part of an archaeological mission undertaken to salvage what little was presumed to remain at the wagon sites before a state pumping project was initiated to divert water from the rapidly rising Great Salt Lake. The pumping project in 1986 threatened destruction of the last remaining evidence of the abandoned Donner-Reed wagons.

Jefferson, T. H. *Map of the Emigrant Road From Independence, Mo., to San Francisco, California.* New York: Berford & Co., 1849. [Published with *Author's Accompaniment*, and an introduction and notes by George R. Stewart, San Francisco: California Historical Society, 1945.]
This excessively rare map (two copies known) not only is "one of the great American maps" in the cartography of the West, but a silent reminder that its author, who vanished after publication, remains an enigma in the history of overland travel.

Kelly, Charles. "Jedediah Smith on the Salt Desert Trail." *Utah Historical Quarterly* 3 (January 1930): 23–27; "The Salt Desert Trail." *Utah Historical Quarterly* 3 (April 1930): 35–52; "The Hastings Cutoff." *Utah Historical Quarterly,* 3 (July 1930): 67–82.
These three articles in the first two numbers of the Utah Historical Quarterly, appear to be "trial balloons" for Kelly's Salt Desert Trails book which was to make its appearance at this time.

————. *Salt Desert Trails: A History of the Hastings Cutoff and Other Early Trails Which Crossed the Great Salt Desert Seeking a Shorter Road to California.* Salt Lake City: Western Printing Company, 1930.
This is a valuable volume for Kelly's early field work.

————. *Old Greenwood: The Story of Caleb Greenwood, Trapper, Pathfinder and Early Pioneer of the West.* Salt Lake City: Western Printing Company, 1936.
Greenwood was an important figure in the overland emigration to California in 1844–1845, and played a role in the relief of the Donner Party.

————. "Gold Seekers on the Hastings Cutoff." *Utah Historical Quarterly* 20 (1952): 3–30; "The Journal of Robert Chalmers April 17–September 1, 1850." *Utah Historical Quarterly* 20 (1952): 31–55.
The first article was written as an addendum to "West From Fort Bridger," published as the 1951 *Utah Historical Quarterly* volume. Kelly was invited to submit this to round out the chronicle of travel on the cutoff following 1846. It is especially interesting because it reflects Kelly's independent point of view, nurtured, of course, during his years of correspondence with his close friends, Dale L. Morgan and J. Roderic Korns. Robert Chalmers was one of a party who crossed the Great Salt Lake Desert one day ahead of a company of three hundred piloted by Auguste Archambault. The Chalmers journal, edited by Kelly, is pertinent to study of the cutoff because it is a parallel account to the early travellers and sheds new information on such landmarks as Adobe Rock in Tooele Valley and seems to verify that Archambault was "freelancing" as a guide while still on Capt. Stansbury's government payroll.

Kelly, Charles, and Dale L. Morgan. *Old Greenwood: The Story of Caleb Greenwood, Trapper, Pathfinder, and Early Pioneer.* Rev. ed. Georgetown: Talisman Press, 1965.
This edition is so extensively revised it must be considered a completely new book. It now is a documentary history of Caleb Greenwood. Only a few paragraphs here and there and the title remain from the original 1936 edition.

Kelly, Charles, and Maurice L. Howe. *Miles Goodyear, First Citizen of Utah, Trapper, Trader and California Pioneer.* Salt Lake City: Western Printing Co., 1937.
This first formal biography of Miles Goodyear, though flawed in the authors' research, provided a significant look at the mountaineer who played a huge role in opening wagon trails to Fort Hall, and by establishing a trading post near the junction of the Ogden and Weber rivers had a part in the founding of Ogden, Utah. He spoke to and influenced many of the principal travelers on the overland trail, including Lienhard, the Donners, Reed, and Brigham Young.

Kenderdine, Thaddeus S. *A California Tramp and Later Footprints; or, Life on the Plains and in the Golden State Thirty Years Ago, with Miscellaneous Sketches in Prose and Verse.* Newtown, PA, 1888.
A Russell, Majors & Waddell teamster who drove across the plains to Great Salt Lake City. In company with a party of Mormon freighters he made the trip to California by way of the Great Sandy Desert to San Pedro.

Kilgore, William H. *The Kilgore Journal of an Overland Journey to California in the year 1850.* Ed. by Joyce Rockwood Muench. New York: Hastings Publishing, 1949.
A brief but colorful visit to Great Salt Lake City in 1850, Kilgore dropped in on the Mormons at the Bowery "built of Dobie Brick, Covered with Plank and Dirted over the top." Kilgore's party took the Fort Hall route, then the Salt Lake road. Whenever possible, Kilgore recorded the names on graves along the road. Interesting journal.

Kittson, William. "Kittson's Journal Covering Peter Skene Ogden's 1824–1825 Snake Country Expedition." Ed. by David E. Miller, *Utah Historical Quarterly* 22 (1954): 125–42.
Kittson was Ogden's chief clerk. Both men kept daily journals of the fur trade and its penetration into present Utah. The journals constitute earliest written descriptions of the area traversed (Cache, Ogden and Weber valleys), and the daily operations of a large company of fur trappers. Journals are earliest written account of northern Utah by eyewitnesses.

Korns, J. Roderic. "West From Fort Bridger: The Pioneering of the Immigrant Trails across Utah, 1846–1850." *Utah Historical Quarterly* 19 (1951).
This scarce volume includes those portions of the James Clyman, Edwin Bryant, Heinrich Lienhard, and James Frazier Reed journals pertinent to Utah. Also the T. H. Jefferson Map, the Golden Pass Road, and Salt Lake Cutoff. Excellently footnoted by Korns and Dale L. Morgan. A new edition is scheduled for publication in 1994 by Utah State University Press.

Lorton, William B. *Over the Salt Lake Trail in the Fall of '49.* Los Angeles: Privately Printed, 1957.
This comprises the text of a letter written by Lorton from Los Angeles, 30 January 1850, and first appeared in the New York Sun and reprinted in the Cleveland Plain Dealer, 11 May 1850. It discusses the departure of Lorton's company from Salt Lake City, 2 October 1849, to California by the Spanish Trail.

Madsen, Brigham D., ed. *A Forty-niner in Utah, with the Stansbury Exploration of Great Salt Lake: Letters and Journal of John Hudson, 1848–50.* Salt Lake City: Tanner Trust Fund, 1981.
A young Englishman, John Hudson, recovering in Great Salt Lake City from an illness that struck him during a crossing of the plains, joined the Mormon Church, and subsequently hired on with Captain Howard Stansbury as a draftsman for the government's survey of the Great Salt Lake.

————, ed. *Exploring the Great Salt Lake: The Stansbury Expedition of 1849–50.* Salt Lake City: University of Utah Press, 1989.
Includes original diaries of principal members of the party, Lt. John W. Gunnison, John Hudson, Albert Carrington, and Stansbury himself. Exhaustive study of journals, maps, letters and other published documents pertaining to the expedition. The diary notations by each member are entered according to date for easy comparison.

Madsen, Steven K. "The Spanish Trail through Canyon Country." *Canyon Legacy* 9 (Spring 1991): 23–29.
Clearly describes the Spanish Trail through southeastern Utah's canyonlands.

Miller, David E. "The First Wagon Train to Cross Utah." *Utah Historical Quarterly* 30 (Winter 1962): 40–51.
From field work supported by a University of Utah research grant, Miller was able to explore and map the various routes of early travelers who crossed Utah before the Mormons. His scholarship resulted in several articles in various journals, including this account as he traced the trail of the Bidwell-Bartleson party from Soda Springs, Idaho, across Utah, to the Humboldt River in Nevada.

————. *Great Salt Lake Past and Present.* Salt Lake City: Utah History Atlas Publisher, 1969.
This booklet was published first in 1949 and reissued with additional material in 1969 as a brief outline for tourists, visitors, and students interested in the lake's history. Its pages contain general information on the recreation, mineral production, salt flat speed attempts, discussions on the several islands in the lake and its bird rookeries, as well as brief summaries on the roles played by Jim Bridger, James Clyman, B.L.E. Bonneville, and John C. Frémont in the history of Great Salt Lake.

Mattes, Merrill J. *Platte River Road Narratives: A Descriptive Bibliography of Travel over the Great Central Route to Oregon, California, Utah, Colorado, Montana, and other Western States and Territories, 1812–1866.* Urbana: University of Illinois Press, 1988.

A distillation of 2,082 accounts of overland travel into highly readable summaries; with each entry rated by the compiler on historical importance and literary value.

Mintz, Lannon W. The Trail: *A Bibliography of the Travelers on the Overland Trail to California, Oregon, Salt Lake City, and Montana during the Years 1841–1864*. Albuquerque: University of New Mexico Press, 1987.
A useful bibliography of 627 published diaries, journals and reminiscences of those who traveled up to two thousand miles west along this overland route.

Morgan, Dale L. *Rand McNally's Pioneer Atlas of the American West.* Historical text by Dale L. Morgan. Chicago: Rand McNally, 1956.
When Rand McNally decided to reprint these maps from the Original Business Atlas of 1876, and discovered there were only a half-dozen copies known to exist in 1955, the company sought out a qualified historian "with a cartographic bent," and Dale L. Morgan was their unanimous choice. The maps of Utah, Wyoming, Nevada, Idaho, Oregon, California, Nebraska, and Montana are especially clear and detailed, each with an accompanying essay by Morgan.

————, ed. *Utah: A Guide to the State.* New York: Hastings House, 1941.
This is perhaps the best volume of the entire American Guide Series, best written, most interesting, most accurate. In the editor's own words, "When Lansford W. Hastings wrote his Emigrant's Guide to Oregon and California, published at Cincinnati, Ohio, in 1845, urging use of the 'Hastings Cutoff,' across the Salt Desert to California, he produced the first guide book to treat even partially the present [1941] area of Utah. This guide to Utah of 1941 is more conservative. One of a series of . . . forty-eight . . . it warns the traveler of rough stretches, quicksands and waterless deserts. Lesser known areas, reached only on shoe or saddle leather, are treated cautiously and factually, without the Hastings bravado."

————, ed. *The Overland Diary of James Pritchard From Kentucky to California in 1849.* Denver: Old West Publishing Co., 1959.
As a diarist, Pritchard was among the earliest to reach California overland in 1849; thus his account is in a few respects unique. Morgan's scholarly research and his travel chart providing dates on which each of the 132 diarists passed each of the 51 trailmarks along the route from St. Louis to Sacramento is invaluable. This volume includes two unpublished maps by J. Goldsborough Bruff and a chart of travel by all known diarists west across South Pass in 1849.

————, ed. *Overland in 1846: Diaries and Letters of the California-Oregon Trail*. Two vols. Georgetown: Talisman Press, 1963.
Diaries and letters for the most part previously unpublished. Craig-Stanley party, first to enter Sacramento Valley with wagons in 1846; Nicholas Carriger who took a variant route from Missouri River to Fort Laramie; diaries of travel from Independence to North Platte and from North Platte to Mission San Jose by the Hastings Cutoff; the Donner Party, pioneering of Hastings and Applegate Cutoffs. All changes in Korns's work of 1951 incorporated in this set by Morgan.

Nunis, Doyce B., Jr., ed. *Josiah Belden, 1841 California Pioneer: His Memoir and Early Letters*. Georgetown: Talisman Press, 1962.
A member of the Bartleson Party, Josiah Belden's manuscripts, recorded for H. H. Bancroft in 1878, and three previously unpublished letters make this an important narrative relating to the first planned overland immigration to California.

————, ed. *The Bidwell-Bartleson Party: 1841 California Emigrant Adventure, Documents and Memoirs of the Overland Pioneers*. Santa Cruz: Western Tanager Press, 1991.
Gathered here for the first time all known firsthand accounts of the Bidwell-Bartleson party, including the elusive second diary of James John.

Overland Journal. Quarterly publication of the Oregon-California Trails Association, Independence, Missouri.
Contains many interesting trail-related papers and book reviews.

Paden, Irene D., ed. *The Journal of Madison Berryman Moorman, 1850–1851*. San Francisco: California Historical Society, 1948.
Journal gives day-by-day description of Moorman's trip to California by the Hastings' Cutoff through Utah and Nevada; however, editor's notes are not entirely accurate and must be regarded with caution.

Platt, P. L., and Nelson Slater. *Traveler's Guide across the Plains upon the Overland Route to California*. San Francisco: John Howell Books, 1963.
Reprinted from the 1852 edition of which only three copies are known. One of the great rarities of Western Americana, this seems to be the work of two men who evidently came overland in different years, Platt in 1849–50, and Slater in 1850–51. Platt had a roadometer attached to his wagon, thus the distances given in this guide are presumed as accurate as those of William Clayton's.

Rucker, Maude A. *The Oregon Trail and Some of Its Blazers.* New York: Walter Neale, 1930.
Contains all available letters, journals and recollections of the Applegates: Lindsay, Jesse, Charles and James. Also reprinted is Jesse Applegate's "A Day With the Cow Column in 1843." Rucker includes first published mention of the existence of a diary by Tamsen Donner, alluded to in a letter by Emerson Hough in which he says he is using the diary and Applegate's journal to write The Covered Wagon, his 1926 novel of overland travel.

Shepard, George. "'O Wickedness, Where is Thy Boundary?': The 1850 California Gold Rush Diary of George Shepard." Introduction by Merrill J. Mattes; notes by David Bigler, Donald Buck, and Merrill J. Mattes. *Overland Journal* 10 (Winter 1992): 2–33.
An important journal of the Pioneer Trail and the Salt Lake Cutoff, with informative notes.

Spedden, H. Rush. "Who Was T. H. Jefferson?" *Overland Journal* 8 (Fall 1990): 2–8.
Highly interesting article on one of 1846's most mysterious travellers; a brilliant mapmaker who seems to have vanished from sight once his work was done. This article includes first publication of an 1871 map showing the Hastings Cutoff route through Skull Valley, and analyzes compass directions described on the T. H. Jefferson map. The author suggests that T. H. Jefferson may have been Tom Hemings Jefferson, son of President Thomas Jefferson and Sally Hemings.

Sullivan, Maurice S., ed. *The Travels of Jedediah S. Smith: A Documentary Outline, Including His Journal.* Santa Ana: Fine Arts Press, 1934.
This pioneering work on Smith is an immediate continuation of the manuscript prepared by Samuel Parkman of Jedediah Smith's travels and adventures. This journal and its predecessor likely are all that remain; it is a certainty the originals were burned long after the death of the fabled mountaineer.

Unruh, John D., Jr. *The Plains Across: The Overland Emigrants and the Trans-Mississippi West, 1840–60.* Urbana: University of Illinois Press, 1979.
Major synthesis of the western emigration. Unruh argues that on the California–Oregon Trail in the 1849–1860 period approximately four hundred Indians died at the hands of emigrants, a higher figure than that for emigrants killed by Indians. White deaths by hostiles has been greatly exaggerated. Of particular value to trail scholars are the author's statistics on such diverse subjects as ratio of oxen to horses to mules in overland travel, and tables showing average travel time in days for the overland journey.

Wagner, Henry R., and Charles L. Camp. *The Plains and the Rockies: A Bibliography of Original Narratives of Travel and Adventure, 1800–1865.* Columbus: Long's College Book Company, 1953.
This third edition of the landmark reference to overland journey is preferred since it fully credits the brilliant historian Dale L. Morgan for his rich contributions mined during years of perusing archives and obscure newspaper files.

Wheat, Carl I. *Mapping the Transmississippi West, 1540–1861.* Five vols. in six. San Francisco: Institute of Historical Cartography, 1957–1963.
A cartographic treasure, describing with bibliographical details, 1,302 maps from 1540 to the Geological Surveys of 1884. Discusses exploration leading to the maps, errors made and discovered; errors undiscovered and copied by subsequent mapmakers.

Index

Abajo Mountains, 17
Adobe Rock, 78, 79
Almo, 108
Antelope Creek, 61
Antelope Island State Park, 47
Antelope Spring, 27
Aragonite, 87
Arches National Park, 16, 18
Ashley, William H., 65

Baker Spring, 51
Bartleson, John, 34, 50, 51
Battle Creek, 40, 47
Beale, Edward F., 22, 23, 30
Bear Creek, 23, 26
Bear River, 36, 38, 39, 40, 41, 42, 61, 62, 63, 102
Beaver Dam Mountains, 31, 32
Beckwith, Lieutenant E.G., 21
Bidwell, John, 34, 35, 39, 41, 43, 44, 45, 46, 48, 49, 51, 53
Bidwell-Bartleson party, 1, 33–53, 91
Bidwell-Bartleson Trail, 33–53
    abandoned wagons, 51
    trail remnant, 51, 52
Bidwell Pass, 53
Big Holes, 19
Big Mountain, 69, 70
Big Rock Candy Mountain, 26
Big Springs, 53
Bigelow Bench, 58, 59, 61
Bigler, Henry, 96, 102, 103, 108

Black Rock, 77
Black's Fork, 59
Blue Spring, 105
Boise Ford, 104
Bonneville Salt Flats, 53, 73
Borrowman, John, 102, 108
Bourdon, Michael, 36, 38
Brewerton, George D., 22, 28
Brannan, Sam, 94, 98
Bridger, Jim, 43, 56, 57, 65, 104
Bridger Butte, 58, 59, 60
Brigham City, 102
Brooks, Noah, 97, 101, 102, 104
Brown, James S., 101
Bruff, J. Goldsborough, 96
Bryant, Edwin, 53, 56, 59, 65, 84, 86, 89
Bryant-Russell party, 3, 4, 34, 58, 59, 60, 61, 62, 63, 66, 68, 69, 75, 79, 85, 91
Burnt Spring, 80, 85
Byrne, Moses, 61, 62

Cache Cave, 58, 64
Cache Valley, 1, 42
California Trail, 74, 94, 109
Call, Anson V., 102
Camp Spring, 31
Cañon Pintado, 12, 14
Canyonlands National Park, 14, 18
Carrington, Albert, 97
Carson, Kit, 22, 28
Carvalho, Solomon, 30
Casa Colorado, 9, 14, 17

Casler, Melyer, 100
Castle Rock, 58, 65
Castle Valley, 21
Cassidy, Butch, 19, 22, 26
Cedar City, 24, 26, 32
Cedar Mountains, 74, 80, 82, 86, 87
Cedar Springs, 46
Cedar Valley, 27
Cement Crossing, 19
City of Rocks, 93, 96, 108, 109
Clayton, William, 56, 64, 65, 71
Clear Creek, 107
Clyman, James, 65, 75, 80, 83
Cobb Peak, 73, 89
Colorado River, 10, 14, 15, 16, 17, 18, 22, 28, 31, 36
Connor, Colonel Patrick E., 31, 36, 40
Connor Springs, 45
Corinne, 44, 45
Courthouse Wash, 16, 18
Coyote Creek, 62, 63
Crane, Addison, 97
Crane Creek, 63
Crescent Junction, 18
Curlew Valley, 106

Delle, 82, 85
Delle Ranch Spring (Cedar Spring), 81
Deseret Peak, 79
DeSmet, Pierre-Jean, 36, 38
Dibble, Jr., Philo, 62
Dinosaur National Monument, 18
Dominguez, Francisco Atanasio, 10, 11
Donner, Tamsen, 81
Donner Hill, 70, 71
Donner Pass, 90
Donner-Reed Memorial Museum, 79
Donner-Reed party, 3, 4, 34, 47, 57, 58, 62, 64, 65, 66, 68, 69, 71, 72, 75, 76, 79, 91
Donner Spring, 34, 52, 90, 91, 92

East Canyon
    Pioneer Trail, 57, 69
    Spanish Trail, 12

East Canyon Creek, 69
East Canyon Reservoir, 66, 68, 69
East Canyon State Park, 68, 69
Echo Canyon, 57, 63, 64
Eightmile Spring, 83
Emigrant Canyon, 96, 108, 109
Emigration Canyon, 4, 57, 70, 72, 76
Enoch, 24, 26, 27
Escalante, Francisco Silvestre Velez de, 10, 11
Escalante Desert, 27
Evanston, 63, 64

Farmington, 100
Fisher, Vardis, 3
Fitzpatrick, Thomas F., 34
Flint, Dr. Thomas, 27
Floating Island, 89, 90
Fort Bridger, 56, 58, 59, 60, 75
Fort Buenaventura State Park, 101
Fort Hall, 36, 38, 46, 56, 74, 94
Frémont, Captain John C., 11, 24, 27, 28, 29, 42, 52, 74, 75, 80, 85, 94
Fremont Junction, 22, 23
Furniture Draw, 21, 22

Garces, Francisco Tomas Hermenegildo, 10
Godbe, William S., 104
Golden Pass Road, 57, 58
Golden Spike National Historic Site, 46
Goodyear, Miles, 57, 100, 101
Grantsville, 74, 76, 77, 78, 79
Grayback Hills, 86, 87, 88, 89
Great Basin, 22, 24, 28, 36, 61
Great Sage Plain, 12, 17
Great Salt Lake, 44, 46, 47, 48, 57, 74, 75
Great Salt Lake Desert, 3, 4, 47, 74, 75, 76, 91
Green, Ephraim, 96, 103
Green River, 10, 14, 16, 17, 18, 36, 59
Green River (town), 10, 18, 22
Gunnison, Captain John W., 16, 19, 21

Halloran, Luke, 77
Hamblin, Jacob, 29, 30
Hampton, Ben, 104
Hampton Ford, 104
Hargraves, John, 77
Harlan-Young party, 3, 4, 34, 58, 62, 66, 75, 77, 91, 94
Hastings, Lansford W., 56, 65, 66, 74, 75, 76, 80, 81, 83, 94
Hastings Cutoff, 3, 73–92, 94
    abandoned wagons, 90
    trail remnant, 82, 90
Hastings Pass, 85, 86
Hatch Wash, 14
Heap, Gwinn Harris, 23, 30
Henry Spring, 83
Hensley, Samuel J., 94, 96, 106
Holmes, Jonathan, 96, 102
Hoppe-Lienhard party, 34, 58, 63, 65, 66, 91
Horseshoe Spring, 81
Hudspeth, James M., 75, 79, 85
Hunt, Jefferson, 24, 27, 28, 32
Huntington, Oliver B., 21

Iosepa, 81
Iron Springs Creek, 27
Ivie Creek, 21
Ivins, Anthony W., 29

Jefferson, T.H., 75, 77, 78, 79, 80, 81, 89, 91
John, James, 35, 39, 41, 42, 43, 45, 47, 48, 49, 51, 52
John Wesley Powell River History Museum, 17, 18, 22
Johnston, Colonel Albert S., 56, 69, 97
Jordan River, 76

Kane Springs, 15, 17
Kelly, Charles, 4
Kelsey, Benjamin, 51
Kelton, 48
Kimball, Hazen, 94, 95, 96
Knight, William H., 65

Knolls, 89
Korns, J. Roderic, 76, 95, 105

Lake Bonneville, 47
LaSal Junction, 14, 17
LaSal Mountains, 15
Leppy Pass, 53
Lienhard, Heinrich, 75, 77, 80, 82, 85, 90, 100
Lincoln Highway, 68, 79
Little Holes, 19, 21, 22
Little Mountain, 70
Little Salt Lake, 11, 24, 26
Locomotive Springs, 48
Long Divide, 42
Looking Glass Rock, 14
Lucin, 52

Mackenzie, Donald, 42
Macomb, Captain John N., 12, 14
Magotsu Creek, 29
Main Canyon, 66, 68
Malad River, 42, 43, 102, 104, 105
May, Richard Martin, 95
Meadow Creek, 28
Moab, 10, 14, 15, 18
Monticello, 12, 14, 17
Morgan, Dale L., 3, 76, 80, 95, 105
Mormon Flat, 69
Mormon Pioneer company, 3, 4, 57, 61, 63, 64, 65, 68, 70, 72
Mountain Meadows, 28, 29, 31, 32
Muddy Creek, 58, 59, 61
Muleshoe Canyon, 15, 17

Needles, The, 55, 62, 63, 64
Newberry, J.N., 14

Oak Spring, 21
Ogden, 66, 101
Ogden River, 101
Oneida Narrows, 33, 39
Oregon Trail, 35, 38, 74
    trail remnant, 36, 38
Oregon Trail State Park, 36
Owl Springs, 51

Parley's Canyon, 58
Paragonah, 24, 26
Park Valley, 50
Parowan Valley, 24, 26
Pilot Peak, 52, 74, 76, 86, 87, 91
Pilot Spring, 106
Pine Valley Mountains, 29
Pinto Creek, 27, 28
Pioneer Trail, 3, 4, 55–72
    trail remnant, 61, 62, 63
Pioneer Trail State Park, 71
Piute Spring, 12
Pony Express stations, 61, 65, 69, 70
Powell, John Wesley, 17, 18
Pratt, Addison, 24, 27, 96, 103, 105, 107, 108
Pratt, Louisa, 101, 103
Pratt, Orson, 64, 68, 70
Pratt, Orville C., 11, 12, 15, 16, 24, 28, 30
Pratt, Parley P., 57, 58
Price, Captain George F., 31
Provost, Étienne, 57

Raft River, 108
Red Creek, 21
Redlum Spring, 74, 80, 81, 82, 83, 84, 85
Reed, James F., 62, 75
Richards, Willard, 102
Rivera, Juan Maria Antonio, 10
Rocky Ford, 42, 43, 105
Rogers, Samuel, 96, 103
Rosebud Springs, 51

St. Louis Rock, 15, 17
Salina, 23, 24
Salina Canyon, 22, 23
Salt Lake City, 72, 77, 98
Salt Lake Cutoff, 3, 93–109
    trail remnant, 107
Salt Lake Valley, 57, 70
Salt Wells, 48
San Rafael Swell, 18, 19, 21, 22
Santa Clara River, 29, 30, 31, 32

Sevier River, 23
Shepard, George, 56, 65, 68, 69, 70, 100
Silver Island Mountains, 73, 89, 90
Silver Zone Pass, 53
Simpson, James H., 97
Skull Valley, 74, 75, 79, 81, 82, 86
Sly, James C., 96
Smith, Azariah, 96, 103, 105
Smith, Jedediah, 4, 10
Snowville, 106
South Canyon, 12
Soda Springs, 1, 34, 35
Spanish Trail, 9–32
    Fish Lake Route, 22, 23, 26
    Southern Route, 11
    trail remnant, 15, 18
Spanish Valley, 15
Stansbury, Captain Howard, 79, 80, 98, 102
Stansbury Mountains, 79
Stowe Creek, 61
Sulphur Creek, 62

Talbot, Lieutenant Theodore, 75
Tenmile Springs, 49
Timpie Spring, 80
Tinaja, La, 14, 17
Trail Spring, 19
Tremonton, 43, 104

Vasquez, Louis, 56
Virgin River, 28, 31

Wasatch Mountains, 68
Weber Canyon, 4, 57, 63, 76
Weber River, 65, 66, 67, 101
Weston Creek, 41
Witches Rocks, 66

Yellow Creek, 62, 63, 64
Young, Brigham, 62, 63, 65, 71, 95, 97

TRAILING THE PIONEERS

~

Designed and composed
by Richard Howe in Adobe Caslon
Trail maps in the narrative by Richard Howe
Endsheet maps by Michael J. Lunt and Kent B. Malan

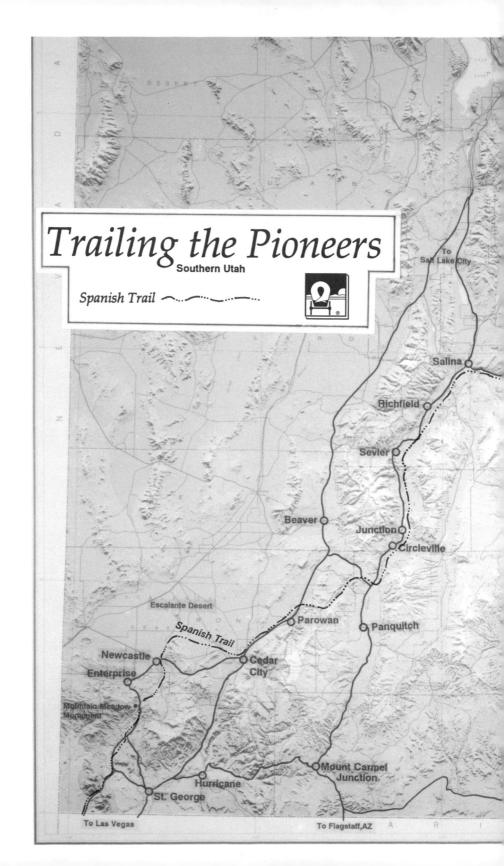

Trailing the Pioneers
Southern Utah

Spanish Trail ~·~·~·~·—·—·

To
Salt Lake City

Salina

Richfield

Sevier

Beaver

Junction

Circleville

Escalante Desert

Spanish Trail

Parowan

Panquitch

Newcastle

Cedar
City

Enterprise

Mountain Meadow
Monument

Mount Carmel
Junction

Hurricane

St. George

To Las Vegas

To Flagstaff, AZ